Wealth God's Way

by
Wilson D. Douglas III

Wealth God's Way

by
Wilson D. Douglas III

Vincom, Inc.
Tulsa, Oklahoma

Unless otherwise indicated, all Scripture quotations are taken from the *King James Version* of the Bible.

The Amplified Bible, New Testament (AMP). Copyright © 1954, 1958 by The Lockman Foundation, La Habra, California.

New American Standard Bible (NASB). Copyright © 1960, 1962, 1963, 1968, 1971, 1972, 1973, 1975, 1977 by The Lockman Foundation, La Habra, California.

Dedication

I dedicate this book to all the members of the Body of Christ seeking balanced and biblically sound truths concerning finances.

Appreciation

My sincere appreciation to the Holy Spirit, who is my Teacher, and to my wife, Elizabeth, and my daugher, Ashley, who are my strong support base.

Also a special, special thanks to the people at Agape Christian Center who have supported the publishing of this book spiritually and financially.

Contents

Introduction

Not long ago, the Lord spoke to me to minister on finances in my church. I had not realized until then that for the past five years, He had been "impregnating" me with His Word on the subject. Then He told me that I was to begin to publish the fruit of that five-year period.

When God is that definite about anything, you just say yes and do not wonder about it. You must simply obey Him, and let Him bring to pass any results. After He spoke to me, I gathered together all of the scriptures I had learned on finances and found there were more than two hundred.

I had not realized that all of the research on the subject that I had done during the past several years would cause the Lord to say, "I need that Word released out of you."

The first thing I saw when I began to run references on finances several years ago is that God always likes the world to know who His people are. Knowing a certain people belonged to *the* God of the universe would enable that people to draw others to Him.

God wants His people to display wealth that the world might know *Him*.

Every time God's people were "showcased" to the world because of prosperity and abundance, it was to reveal the goodness of God — from Abraham on through the scriptures. However, if they were not living the life that allowed God to bless them, Israel did not get the prosperity with which to display His goodness.

The way the world recognizes God's people is because of how they are blessed. Our witnesses as people of God, "the light of the world" today (Matt. 5:14), must be more than saying, "I love the Lord. I am saved and going to Heaven."

There should be some evidence flowing out of your life that shows your God is not a "welfare" God, that He is not poor but owns the earth and all of its resources. (Ps. 24:1.) God is above welfare, higher than social security, and able to provide more than food stamps. Most Christians live below their privileges, partly because of lack of knowledge and partly because they choose to live that way.

Many pastors have been hesitant to teach on finances because of the recent wave of hostility in this country toward the people of God who have high standards of living. We did not want to appear greedy or arrogant, and many of us fell into false humility. We have allowed the devil to steal blessings from us and from our people, blessings that are our rightful inheritance in Jesus.

Also, the media for the past two or three years has been trying to reinforce the Middle Ages' concept that all Christians should be poor. If Christians fall in line with this antagonism toward prosperity for us, we will never be able to take the Gospel all over the earth so that the end can come. (Matt. 24:14.)

The devil has used the lie that spirituality involves poverty to defeat God's people, to cause us to retreat instead of taking back more territory from him. The

Gospel is not being preached as it should be. People are dying and going to hell because few Christians or Christian groups have enough money to go win them.

We must learn not to let the faces of the world and "religious" Christians intimidate us from speaking out truths that may not be popular. Ezekiel knew that whatever he said that was not right, or whatever he did not say that he should have, would cause the blood of the people to be on his hands. (Ezek. 33:7-9.)

The Lord showed me in First Chronicles 21:1-27 where David fell into the devil's trap of numbering the children of Israel, and seventy thousand people died. His decision caused parents to lose loved ones and brought great grief and pain to the nation. His choice did not affect only himself.

No one is an island set aside, so that every decision only affects him or her. Everything we do affects other people. So pastors who do not preach that God's blessings include finances are hurting the "sheep" God has placed in their care.

Of course, motives for seeking wealth are of extreme importance. We need to learn a lesson from Solomon. We do not ask God for wealth to spend on our own lusts. (James 4:3.) But we can believe His promises to meet our needs (Philip. 4:19), to rebuke the devourer (Mal. 3:11), and to give us seed for sowing. (2 Cor. 9:10.) We can have faith that His principles are true and always work.

If we ask Him for wisdom (revelation through His Word) and a fellowshipping knowledge of the Trinity, then God will add wealth and honor. We will then be in line to receive covenant blessings. God's blessing of Solomon was a sign that David's son had God's approval. And there was not another king like him in his day. The Bible says he exceeded all the other kings.

> So king Solomon exceeded all the kings of the
> earth for riches and for wisdom.
>
> And all the earth sought to Solomon, to hear his
> wisdom, which God had put in his heart.
>
> And the king made silver to be in Jerusalem as
> stones, and cedars made he to be as the sycomore trees
> that are in the vale, for abundance.
>
> 1 Kings 10:23,24,27

God says it is time to remove the lie that proverty
equals spirituality. If that were true, the homeless
people on the street would be the closest to God of
any people! It is time to bring forth the truth that you
get not only what you believe and speak forth, but that
pastors get what they teach. The Bible says all things are
possible with God *if we just believe*. (Matt. 19:26.)

The Lord wants me to share things that will enable
readers to give birth to finances in their lives. It is my
prayer that these concepts from the Word of God will
make a substantial difference in the lives of everyone
who reads this book.

If You Don't See It, You Can't Receive It

The author of Hebrews wrote: **Now faith is the
substance of things *hoped* for . . .** (Heb. 11:1). You
cannot ''hope'' on nothing. If there is no basis for
hope, faith cannot work. If the most you ever dream
of for yourself and your family is a weekly paycheck,
that is all you will ever get. You must dream past
Friday.

*If you cannot see a blessing in your mind, you cannot
receive it.*

You must dream past that second-hand car, that
rental house or apartment, that used furniture. And
you must understand first of all that the one who

brings dreams to pass is God. He is the One Who takes impossibilities and makes them possible.

The Apostle Paul wrote that **faith cometh by hearing and hearing by the word** (Rom. 10:17). If you never vocalize what you are dreaming, you will never see it, never have faith for it.

David told Solomon, ''You are going to build a house for God Almighty. I am going to be gathered to my fathers, but you are to sit on my throne and build a house for God. You are going to lead God's people.'' (1 Chron. 28:1-10.)

Solomon began to envision leading God's people, and he knew he would need some help. That night God appeared to Solomon and said:

. . . Ask what I shall give thee.

And Solomon said unto God, Thou hast shewed great mercy unto David my father, and hast made me to reign in his stead.

Now, O Lord God, let thy promise unto David my father be established: for thou hast made me king over a people like the dust of the earth in multitude.

Give me now wisdom and knowledge, that I may go out and come in before this people: for who can judge this thy people, that is so great?

And God said to Solomon, Because this was in thine heart, and thou hast not asked riches, wealth, or honour, nor the life of thine enemies, neither yet hast asked long life; but hast asked wisdom and knowledge for thyself, that thou mayest judge my people, over whom I have made thee king:

Wisdom and knowledge is granted unto thee; and I will give thee riches, and wealth, and honour, such as none of the kings have had that have been before thee, neither shall there any after thee have the like.

2 Chronicles 1:7-12

God's Word works in cooperation with your intelligence to produce godly wisdom. So do not put your brain in mothballs when you get saved. We have been taught not to use our imaginations in the Church, but you must be able to envision yourself being prosperous. If you cannot believe that God loves you and wants you blessed, then you cannot *see* prosperity for yourself.

If you cannot see this, you will have no grounds for hoping things will be different in your circumstances. If you want to be defeated, do not dare to dream. Do not dare to think of owning your own company. Do not dare to think of getting a good job, or going back to school and getting off welfare.

Do you ever see yourself writing out a check to some ministry for ten thousand dollars?

To say such things are impossible is to say that God is not big enough to deal with *your* problem. That is almost blasphemy! If God is not bigger than your circumstances, you really are in trouble.

Perhaps you are wondering whether God really wants us to be blessed. So let me show you from His Word what His will is for His people. Here is what He told Israel after He got them out of Egyptian bondage:

> Now therefore, if ye will obey my voice indeed, and keep my covenant, then ye shall be a peculiar treasure unto me above all people: for all the earth is mine:
>
> And ye shall be unto me a kingdom of priests, and an holy nation. . . .
>
> Exodus 19:5,6

"But," you may say, "that was for the twelve tribes of Israel. That was under the Old Covenant."

We Have a Better Covenant

The author of Hebrews wrote that entire book to *prove* that we, the elect of the New Covenant, have a *better* covenant than the natural descendants of Abraham. We also are called "a holy nation," and "kings and priests."

> But ye are a chosen generation, a royal priesthood, *an holy nation,* a *peculiar people* (treasure); that ye should shew forth the praises of him who hath called you out of darkness into his marvellous light.
>
> 1 Peter 2:9

> And (Jesus) hath made us kings and priests unto God and his Father; to him be glory and dominion for ever and ever. Amen.
>
> Revelation 1:6

In addition, through the blood covenant ratified by Jesus on the cross, we also are Abraham's descendants. Therefore, we are to be recipients of the blessings of the Old Covenant fulfilled and improved in the New.

> For ye are all the children of God by faith in Christ Jesus.
>
> For as many of you as have been baptized into Christ have put on Christ.
>
> There is neither Jew nor Greek, there is neither bond nor free, there is neither male nor female: for ye are all one in Christ Jesus.
>
> And if ye be Christ's, then are ye Abraham's seed, and heirs according to the promise.
>
> Galatians 3:26-29

Second Corinthians 8:9 says that Jesus became poor in order that all who accept Him as Savior might be rich. Paul did not write that Jesus became poor that we might remain poor. *Rich* means having my needs met, my bills paid in full, and an abundance left over to give for the spreading of the Gospel and to those who are in need. Paul was talking about *rich* in all areas — spirit, soul, and body.

When you are the head and not the tail, as God told Israel, (Deut. 28:13), you are up where everyone can see you. Jesus said we were as a "city set on a hill." (Matt. 5:14.)

Receiving the blessings starts with being able to see and believe that God loves you and that He wants you to be blessed. God did not love Solomon more than He loves you — for whom His Son died on the cross, was buried, and resurrected from the dead.

God showed His gratitude to Solomon because in his early days as king, he was obedient and had the right attitude in his heart. In his latter years, as we know, he strayed away from God, which cost his son the united kingdom. However, God does not bless you on what you are *going* to do, but on where you are right now.

You cannot beat God at giving. He appreciates it when you obey and do what He asks you to do. When God shows gratitude, everyone around you knows it, because you are placed above, not below. They will not have any doubt who your God is. When they talk to you about your prosperity, you will have an opportunity to witness to them.

There will never be people asking a raggedy, homeless, street person, "Who is your God?"

I heard Fred Price tell once of being out on the street in his Rolls Royce (which his congregation took up a collection to buy as a love gift for him) when someone walked up to him and asked, "What are you pushing?"

Brother Price replied, "I'm 'pushing' Jesus."

He pointed out that if he had been driving a second-hand ordinary car, no one ever would have asked him that question. He also says that by dressing nicely and driving an expensive car, he gets to witness to executives. When you get the man at the top saved, the knowledge of Jesus can filter down.

God says, ''I want to bless My children so that I can put them on display. When non-believers ask how they got so blessed, My children can testify of Me.''

When you get to the place where you can see prosperity for yourself through Jesus, enough for hope to spring up in your heart, then you are ready to begin the steps on the path to receiving financial blessings. At that point, the next thing God wants to know — and that you need to know about yourself — is this:

If you get wealth, what are you going to do with it? You need to know the purpose of wealth in order to properly disperse it and maintain the blessings.

Wilson D. Douglas III, Pastor
Agape Christian Center
League, Texas

1
Faith Works by Love

Once you see that God desires you to prosper financially and that having more than enough to meet your needs is your right and privilege through Jesus — and once you see that whatever God gives you is not to keep but to use for Him — you are ready to find out how to be in a place where financial blessings can flow *to* you.

If simply being saved and becoming a part of the blood covenant brought you the blessings as it does eternal life, all Christians automatically would be well-to-do. However, God's kingdom does not work that way. He gives us what we cannot do for ourselves, but some things that are ours by right involve attitudes and actions on our part. That is how we mature in God.

God will not always carry us as babies. If we do not mature in Him, we cannot fully do His work. (Heb. 5:12-14.) We cannot conform to the image of Jesus (Rom. 8:29) without changing and growing. Therefore, for the blessings of the covenant, we are required to do some things: basically, *hear and obey*. (Deut. 13:4.)

However, "hearing and obeying" involve a lot of things. Hearing means studying the written Word of God, being part of a good church where the Word of God is taught and can be heard, and being able to

1

"hear" the Holy Spirit through a witness or "the still, small voice," or through "knowing that you know" — a peace in your inner man. (James 3:15-17.)

Obedience is not simply "doing what you are told" in legalistic attitudes. Obedience means conforming to Jesus in all areas — spirit, soul, and body. However, even obedience can become "religion" and not accomplish maturity in you *without faith.*

Faith has been taught extensively and in depth in some circles of the Church for the past twenty years or more. But faith also, in some churches and some people, has been turned into "formulas." Some even have gotten into presumption and called their attitudes "faith." At this point, I feel many of us need to back up and take another look at what faith really means.

Faith simply is *believing* that something is true. You believe God is God, and that by accepting Jesus, you will become a child of God and have eternal life with Him. That is how you get saved. Then, because of your belief, you begin to confess Jesus to those around you. (Rom. 10:9,10.) That is the first step to maturing in the kingdom.

The second step is the key to continuing to mature, receiving financial and other covenant blessings, and being able to be used of God. That second step is learning this truth: *Faith works by love.* Faith without a humble, reverential love of God and a genuine love for your brothers and sisters in Him will eventually turn into a dead, religious attitude in your heart.

> **For in Jesus Christ neither circumcision availeth any thing, nor uncircumcision; *but faith which worketh by love.***
> **Galatians 5:6**

Let me say it another way: *Without love, your faith will not work.*

If you love your fellow citizens in the kingdom, you will not judge them, you will not talk about them — and your faith will work.

And this commandment have we from him, That he who loveth God love his brother also.
1 John 4:21

So you see, loving your brothers and sisters in the Body of Christ is a prerequisite to loving God and is a *commandment* from Jesus. No wonder faith only works by love!

It does not matter if you were born in a ten-foot hole in the ground with dirt on you. You can rise up out of there, and God will help you get on top of the mountain. But you must *think* right. Many Christians cannot expect to be prosperous, because they have been taught that it is not good for them to have a lot of money. They have been taught that money itself is evil.

If you believe that — and in the previous chapters, I have shown you from the Bible that those ideas are false — then how can you have faith to receive?

And how can you love other people when your own life is miserable and poor and lacking even your needs met? You will find most people in the poverty level of society are bitter, resentful, and even full of hatred of others.

No matter how badly off you are right now, repent of any such attitudes and ask God to give you a love for your brothers and sisters in Him. Begin to make choices to love others. Love is a choice, anyway, not a feeling. The feelings will follow the choices.

Choose to love others in order that your faith may work for you and for them.

If you read the four gospels carefully, you will find that everything Jesus did flowed out of His love for the Father and for others. The miracles He did were rooted in a great love and compassion for the hurting, the downtrodden, and the poor. When He was not preaching and teaching, most of His time was spent with those people, not with the religious people of His day.

Jesus Worked by Love

When Jesus taught in the synagogue at Nazareth, His hometown, He quoted a passage from Isaiah:

The Spirit of the Lord is upon me, because he hath anointed me to preach the gospel to the poor; he hath sent me to heal the brokenhearted, to preach deliverance to the captives, and recovering of sight to the blind, to set at liberty them that are bruised,

To preach the acceptable year of the Lord.

Luke 4:18,19

He was reading from Isaiah 61, but He stopped in the middle of the second verse. The next phrase would have been **and the day of vengeance of our God,** and it was not time for that day to be preached yet. What He meant, when He said, **This day is this scripture fulfilled in your ears** (Luke 4:21), was this:

*I have been anointed by God to preach the good news to those who are in poverty. The "good news" is that, through Me, they do not have to remain poor.

*I have been sent to the brokenhearted, to heal them so they no longer are depressed and sorrowful.

*I have been sent to set free those in bondage to the devil and those who are bruised.

*I have been sent to restore sight to the blind and hearing to the deaf.

*I have been sent to tell you that *this* is the time foretold of the prophets when God would again visit His people with healing in His wings.

All of the things Jesus quoted from Isaiah's prophecy were to be turned around, reversed, by Him. If He reversed physical handicaps, demonic oppression and possession, and all of the other things mentioned, why would one thing be left unturned? Yet that is what Christians are taught.

In essence, what we have been taught is that Jesus said He came to defeat the works of the devil (1 John 3:8), but poverty was too much for Him. He restored all of the blessings of the covenant except the material ones. Everything He did was in the spiritual realm.

Nearly all churches used to teach, and some still do, that even physical healing was not meant by Jesus when He proclaimed His mission in the synagogue at Nazareth. *He* did those things on earth, and the early apostles did some miracles. However, some say, when the apostles all died, there was no more provision in the atonement for anything in the natural.

Many of us today laugh at how ridiculous that sounds — yet we still have the same thinking about finances! We separate one thing from a series of things Jesus Himself said He came to do and say one thing was left out. Religion says all of Satan's works were defeated — except poverty.

However, the Bible shows that Jesus defeated *all* of the works of Satan, and He came to do that because of the love of God for us. (John 3:16.) Before we were saved, God loved us. (Eph. 2:4,5.) And if Jesus had not loved the Father more than Himself and mankind more than His life, could He have given up His riches to become ''poor''? Could He have suffered the death

He did in order for us to be rich *in every area of our lives?* (2 Cor. 8:9.)

We are not told specifically in the Bible that Jesus did this or that miracle through love. However, if you read about His character and you read about His miracles with spiritual understanding, you cannot help but see that He loved those people and had a great compassion for them.

Jesus operated by faith when He was on earth. His miracles were not done by some supernatural force that sprang out of His fingertips. He *believed* that God would resurrect Him from the dead, if He followed through on the assignment for which He came to earth.

His faith was rooted in love, however. That is how it worked — not because He was the Son of God, but because He loved the Father and He loved mankind. There was nothing He did while on earth that we cannot do (John 14:12), *but we must do these things the same way He did:* by faith working through love.

When Jesus multiplied the loaves and fishes, He did it because He loved that multitude of people and felt a great compassion for their hunger and thirst. Incidentally, the people were in a position to receive the miracle because they loved hearing the Word so much they were willing to sleep outdoors and sit through a three-day service without food.

> **And Jesus went forth, and saw a great multitude, and was moved with compassion toward them . . . .**
> **Matthew 14:14**

Matthew then proceeded to tell how Jesus healed the sick, and at the end of the day multiplied the five loaves and two fishes in order to feed five thousand men, besides women and children. In the next chapter, Matthew writes of a second time when Jesus multiplied food for the people out of *compassion,* which means "love and caring."

> Then Jesus called his disciples unto him, and said, I have *compassion* on the multitude, because they continue with me now three days, and have nothing to eat: and I will not send them away fasting, lest they faint in the way.
>
> Matthew 15:32

He did not look at the fact that there was only enough food for one person. He looked up at the Father, blessed the food, then broke the bread and fish into pieces — and kept breaking and breaking until everyone had all they wanted and baskets were left over. His *faith* saw the multitudes, on whom He had *compassion* (whom He loved), as already fed. He called things which were not as though they were, (the same principle Abraham operated on through faith — Rom. 4:17), and because of His love, faith worked the miracles.

Jesus taught that the two greatest commandments were to love God with your whole heart and your neighbor as yourself. (Matt. 22:38-40.) Then He gave His disciples (we are His modern-day disciples) *a new commandment.* What He told them was intended for His entire Body down through the centuries.

> A new commandment I give unto you, That ye love one another; as I have loved you, that ye also love one another.
>
> By this shall all men know that ye are my disciples, if ye have love one to another.
>
> John 13:34,35

Without faith working through love, all of the teaching on prosperity that you can hear will do you no good. You must believe that it is yours, you must be able to see yourself having it, and you must love

God and your fellow Christians enough to give it away after you have it.

If you still have a problem thinking we are supposed to be like Jesus, yet Jesus was poor while on earth, then you need to understand that Jesus did not live a poverty-stricken life while on earth. He lived a *simple* life, with a simple lifestyle — according to the years of His life we know about. But He was not in poverty.

Jesus Did Not Live in Poverty

Jesus is the Head, and we are His Body, the Apostle Paul wrote in several of his epistles. (1 Cor. 11:3; Eph. 1:22, 4:15; 5:23; Col. 1:18, 2:10,19.) We need to understand that *as the Head goes, so goes the Body.* Your wealth is tied up with Jesus, because you are connected to Him.

When Paul wrote that Jesus came to earth exchanging His riches for our poverty in order that we might be rich, he was writing to a people who understood "covenant language." Two parties to a blood covenant exchanged ownership of everything.

Jesus exchanged His robe of righteousness for the filthy rags of our sins. He became a sin-offering for us. (Heb. 9:28, 10:5-12.) He took our name, Man, and gave us His name, Christian, and so forth. If He exchanged with us, why do we still have to keep our old things? We give up the sin nature when we get His righteousness, for example.

He did not become a sin offering so that we could be like Him in that. He became a sin offering so *that we would not have to experience spiritual death for our sins.* Therefore, He did not become "poor" so that we could live poverty-stricken lives and be spiritual because we are poor. That is the exact opposite of what a "covenant-exchange" means.

Even if His becoming "poor" meant He lived a mean, miserable, poverty-ridden life, it also would mean He did that so that we could live the total opposite way — rich, comfortable, and happy. However, I can show you from the scriptures that He did not live without means.

He did not live in the lap of luxury, squandering wealth on carnal lusts — but then neither are we supposed to. But He did always have everything He needed, money to pay His bills, and money and food to give. That is the "abundant life," as far as I can tell from the Word of God.

So Jesus lived simply but abundantly with all of His needs met. That is the example we are to follow. The main reason Jesus was not poor was because *everything on earth was at His disposal* through faith working by love. Let me give you some proof that Jesus did not walk in lack:

*During His ministry, Jesus had so many funds that He had a treasurer — Judas Iscariot. (John 13:29.) There was enough money given to Jesus and the disciples that Judas could steal from it and what he took apparently not be missed. (John 12:4-6.)

Incidentally, the situation with Judas shows me that you can be called of God, answer the call, not be living right, and still have an anointing. When the disciples were sent to cast out devils, lay hands on the sick, and so forth, *all twelve* went and came back rejoicing. The Bible does not say they all went except Judas.

In fact, on the Day of Pentecost, Peter specifically said that, before he betrayed Jesus, Judas had been "numbered" with the disciples and **had obtained part of this ministry** (Acts 1:16-20).

However, you cannot continue to get away forever with not living right, so it is always dangerous to trample on the grace of God and take His mercy for granted. Sooner or later, you will cross the line of mercy, as Judas did, and consequences will follow: **For the wages of sin is death** (Rom. 6:23).

The point is: Just because someone is operating in the gifts of the Holy Spirit and doing miracles is no sign their lives are in order. Being used by God and becoming mature in conforming to the image of Jesus are two different things. One is the work you do *for* God; the other is personal spiritual growth. And you grow by changing and changing and changing from the old nature to the new, not through your works.

*As the "second man" (Adam being the "first" man, from whom all of the natural race are descended), Jesus (from whom all those of the new birth are "descended") had dominion over everything on earth. (1 Cor. 15:27.) So did the first Adam — until He fell. (Gen. 1:26-29.) Jesus never fell short of the glory of God. He never failed one time in hearing the Father and obeying.

Jesus could multiply the fish, because He had authority over them. He could multiply bread, because He had dominion over plants and herbs. He took authority over what was under His dominion. God said the earth was His and the fullness thereof. (Ps. 24:1.) Then in another place, He said the earth — meaning the rule over it — belongs to the children of men. (Ps. 115:16.)

The "prime directive" for mankind as children of God was to "be fruitful, multiply, subdue the earth, and have dominion." (Gen. 1:28.)

Everything was at Jesus' disposal *if He believed* (had faith) and walked in authority. However, without also being total love, His faith would not have worked.

*How could He be poor when He could take authority over the elements? He stopped storms, calmed seas, and walked on water.

*How could He be poor when He had authority over *all* power of the enemy? Satan could not put sickness, disease, or poverty on Him. *That* is riches. Satan could not even kill Him. He said that He laid down His own life. (John 10:17,18.)

*When His taxes came due, all He had to do was send Peter to look in a fish's mouth. (Matt. 17:24-27.) He did not have to spend money out of His treasury. Jesus always walked in abundance.

*Even if He did not own a house (Matt. 8:20), He may have rented one, because the Bible talks about Him returning to His "home" in Capernaum during His ministry. (Matt. 4:13-16.) In Mark 2:1 in the story of the man with palsy let down from the roof, the Bible says, **and it was noised that he was in the house.** And in Mark 9:33, again it says **and being in the house.** Apparently, He had made that city His headquarters, and the people knew what "the house" meant. He always had a place to stay when He needed it.

*As far as clothes went, apparently He wore the best. When Jesus was crucified, He was wearing a robe of such good quality that rather than tear it, the Roman soldiers cast dice for it. (Mark 15:24.) For Romans to want it, that must have been a very expensive robe!

Jesus knew His needs would be met. He knew His Father owned everything, and He could have it all. Yet He always remained humble, and He never asked anything selfishly. The devil tried to tempt Him with hunger once (Matt. 4:1-4), but He confidently waited for His Father to feed Him. (Matt. 4: 11.) He never got into presumption and turned stones into bread, even after forty days' fasting.

When you can follow Jesus' example, stay humble, and not get into presumption to satisfy the body or the soul, God will bless you with abundance.

When you forget where your help comes from, wealth will take wings and fly away.

When you forget to love your neighbor as you love yourself, your faith will not work in any area.

What you must do is let the Holy Spirit help you lay a proper foundation for receiving wealth.

2
Who Owns the Wealth of the World?

It is important to have a good, solid foundation, if you are going to build a lasting structure of any kind. If you build a house on sand, it will not last very long. But if you dig deep into the earth and find a rock on which to build, when the storms of life come, your "house will stand."

When you have done all you can to stand, you will still be standing (Eph. 6:13) — *if* you build on a firm foundation.

In order to keep your attitude and your motives toward wealth straight in the Lord, you must understand clearly *who owns all of it*. If you slip into thinking that *you* own what is given to you by God, sooner or later, you will misuse or abuse what you have.

When you know who owns something, and you know you only have the use of it as long as you take good care of it, then you are more likely to be careful with that thing. You are less likely to be careful with something you own than with something *loaned* to you to use. You are less likely to be stingy with something temporarily yours than if you get possession of it.

13

When I began to minister this teaching in my church, the Lord said to me, "Let them know they do not own anything."

The reason many people have not been walking in close fellowship with God is because they think the money they receive is theirs.

Christians think, "It's my paycheck, my possessions, my job, my car, my house, my clothes," and so forth.

Actually, *you* do not own anything. You were "bought with a price" by Jesus on the cross.

The mature Christian considers himself, or herself, a "bondslave" of Jesus Christ (Rom. 1:1), just as the Apostle Paul did. (The *King James Version* translates that "servant," but the original Greek word is *bondslave*.) So in truth, everything you own *He* owns.

However, most of the time, when God says, "Give me something back that I 'loaned' you, or let you use for a time," we get very upset. Before I ever became a tither, I learned that I do not own anything.

In Psalm 24:1, the Lord said *He* owned the earth, and not only the planet, but everything on it. If He owns it, where does that put you? That makes you simply a steward, one who has authority or dominion (rule) over something *on behalf of the owner*.

Everything on this earth literally is "on loan" to man from God, and everyone will be called to give an account of his, or her, stewardship in the final judgment.

You do not even own yourself. What makes you think you can run around and do anything you want with your body when you do not even own it? Once you are born again, your body is the temple of God, a dwelling place for the Holy Spirit who has made you a new creature in Christ Jesus. (2 Cor. 5:17.)

Before you were born again, you belonged to Satan, who stole dominion over the earth and its beings from Adam and Eve. Jesus paid the price and, as the "last Adam," the "second man" (1 Cor. 15:45), He regained dominion, as I explained in the last chapter. However, unless you *accept* Jesus as your Redeemer (one who "redeems" something from someone else), you are still under the authority of the old "owner."

No one who has lived on earth (or who will live on earth) ever belonged to himself or herself.

You either are the property of Satan or the property of God Almighty. God gave man the ability and the right to make choices, but all of your choices — little or big — simply reflect which owner you are choosing.

There are many scriptures which tell you this, but look at just one passage, Psalm 104:24-29:

> **O Lord, how manifold** (many and varied) **are thy works! in wisdom hast thou made them all: the earth is full of** *thy* **riches.**
>
> **So is this great and wide sea, wherein are things creeping innumerable, both small and great beasts.**
>
> **There go the ships: there is that leviathan, whom thou hast made to play therein.**
>
> **These wait all upon thee; that thou mayest give them their meat in due season.**
>
> **That thou givest them they gather: thou openest thine hand, they are filled with good.**
>
> **Thou hidest thy face, they are troubled: thou takest away their breath, they die, and return to their dust.**

If God did not own the earth and everything on it, He could not legally have cleansed it of everything but those people, animals, and things in Noah's ark. Mankind was only given the right to rule over it and, as the "other side of the coin," the responsibility to take care of the earth and everything on it.

If God did not own everything, He could not have legally given Abraham's descendants a specific piece of land as their country. Even then, the Israelites knew the land itself belonged to God and was only in their care.

Christians need to get this firmly in their mind in order to detach themselves from all earthly possessions, even *self*. If you "know that you know that you know" that you do not own anything, not even yourself, it is easier to give it away. That understanding makes it easier to let the Holy Spirit have authority over your time as well as your ways.

All the earth is full of *His* riches, not yours.

When you understand that everything in heaven and earth belongs to God, the Maker and Creator, then you can walk in blessings. Then *yours* is the kingdom. When you understand that riches and honor both come from God, then you are ready to be used fully by God. After that, the riches and honor will come from Him to you for *His* glory.

You Need God To "Open His Hand"

David knew very clearly who owns everything. This truth is included in many of his psalms to the Lord. He stated it again in his announcement to Israel that he had gathered all the materials to build the temple — but that Solomon was the one who would build it. (1 Chron. 29:1-10.)

Here are two verses from David's prayer to the Lord on that day.

> Thine, O Lord, is the greatness, and the power, and the glory, and the victory, and the majesty: for all that is in the heaven and in the earth is thine; thine is the kingdom, O Lord, and thou art exalted as head above all.

> Both riches and honour come of thee, and thou reignest over all; and in thine hand is power and might; and in thine hand it is to make great, and to give strength unto all.
>
> 1 Chronicles 29:11,12

In Psalm 145:16, David sang about God opening His hand. And, unless God opens His hand to you, you would have nothing. He gives the sun, rain, seasons, and cycle of growth for crops and trees to all mankind. He said He caused it to rain on the just and the unjust alike. (Matt. 5:45.) That is simply His goodness and provision for His creations.

The only exception is when a people or a nation have trampled on His mercy to the extent that He can no longer withhold judgment. The consequences (curses) can be held back no longer, either because there is no person to stand in the gap (Ezek. 22:30), or because the wickedness is so great, no one *can* stand in the gap. (Isa. 22:14.)

Just before God closed His hand on everything for those peoples, He tried to give them a final warning by "causing it to rain on one city and not another," or bringing famine on one place and abundance on the one next door. (Amos 4:6-11.) He did this — and will continue to do this throughout history — to try to get their focus on Him, whose opening and closing hand controls all blessings.

However, there are blessings for His covenant children above and beyond the everyday workings of the earth and the meeting of needs. Those come to you when God opens His hand for you. Conversely, if God's hand is closed to you because of your attitude, motives, or behavior, then you will not receive anything from Him.

We will talk about tithing in another chapter, but I will tell you that, as a child of God, not tithing and not giving offerings will close God's hand to you. You may pay off all your natural debts and think you are debt free, but if you have not given what God said to give — then you are still in debt.

Think about what being in debt means: If you do not pay that mortgage, that note, that time payment, the owner of those notes can come and take what you have away from you. If you do not pay the gas, water, or lights, the company can take that service away from you.

So what happens when you owe God? He has the right to take those things away from you. He only asks for ten percent back to keep His work going. If you genuinely understand the concept of being a bondservant, and you commit to that, He will ask you from time to time to give things to other people. However, most of the time, He allows you to use and enjoy the rest.

If He closes His hand, however, you will lose the things He has blessed you with. The sad part is that we do not object to paying up to twenty-some percent sometimes to have the use of money or to gain possessions. But we object to returning to God the small percentage of His own resources.

Giving should not be a big deal for Christians. They only gain when they give. That is one of God's laws: the law of sowing and reaping which works the same in all areas of life. You are only investing in — and getting the use of — things that already belong to God.

You cannot afford not to give. That will box you in until Jesus comes. You will barely get along in life.

God says to us, "I own everything, but I will give you up to a hundred percent interest when you loan Me back some of what already is Mine."

In David's message to the Israelites the day he talked about the building of the temple, he also said:

> **O Lord our God, all this store that we have prepared to build thee an house for thine holy name cometh of thine hand, and is all thine own.**
> **1 Chronicles 29:16**

He understood that, even though the gold, silver, wood, iron, brass, precious stones, and so forth, had been given by the people and by the kings of surrounding nations as tribute, all of it really belonged to God. He knew that God had given those things *to* those people in order for them to have things to contribute *to* the temple.

Why does God want to bless His people with things? Partly because He loves us, and partly because — as I mentioned in the Introduction — He wants the world to see who He is through us. It does not bring glory to God for His people to be broke, poor, living on welfare and food stamps, and driving old beat-up cars.

The Bible says we are to be the *light* of the world, not live in darkness. As long as you live in this world, money is important. (Eccl. 10:19.) As long as you understand it is a "means to an end" and do not love money for itself, you are not in bondage to it.

You need money to live in this world's systems, and God wants you to have it. God owns wealth we do not even know about yet. The Lord showed me that all of the wealth He owns that no one knows about yet is going to be revealed to His people. (Isa. 45:3.)

This is why you cannot look to your job as your source of income. In the meantime, while you are laying this foundation for being blessed, and believing in faith through love, *take care of what you do have.* If you gave someone something, and they misused or abused it, would you give them anything else? Then why would you think God would do that?

After God provided all of the wealth and materials for Solomon to build the temple, He allowed it to be destroyed when the people lost sight of who He was and that His temple should be honored and taken care of as in the beginning.

After Judah spent seventy years in exile and returned to Jerusalem, the Lord spoke through the prophet Haggai and said:

> **Who is left among you that saw this house in her first glory? and how do ye see it now? is it not in your eyes in comparison of it as nothing?**
>
> **Haggai 2:3**

God let Babylon destroy the temple, because Judah — the remnant of Israel — began walking in sin and disobedience. That closes God's hand. Not taking care of what He gives you also will close His hand.

Make a good showing for God with what you have. Keep that vehicle clean and in good repair, keep that house and yard as clean as possible, and make what you have last as long as you can. If you only have one pair of jeans and one shirt, keep them washed and mended. Do not dress and act as if you do not have anything.

Also, I do not wear "faddish" dress styles. Fads fade, and usually, those are "exhibitionist" clothes. They are designed to draw attention to *you*. I believe it is better to wear nice, well-cut and well-designed clothes that complement your looks rather than things that draw attention to your looks.

It is one thing to look as if you honorably represent the Kingdom of God, and it is another to be a Christian, yet look as if you are representing the world. Wearing extreme fashions simply because they are the latest fad represents the world, not God.

Do Not Bring Reproach on God

Christians are terrible about trying to get sympathy, about acting as if they deserve more help because they are "poor Christians," trying to do the Lord's will. What kind of impression of your owner and heavenly Boss does that give the world?

In Galatians 5:22,23, where the fruits of the Spirit are listed, I cannot find self-pity anywhere! In fact, self-pity and failure in your life bring reproach on God.

If the furniture store sends a truck to pull up in front of your house and take back your television set or your furniture and appliances, that does not make a good testimony to Almighty God. Too many Christians operate in a "poverty mentality," one that goes around saying or implying, "poor me."

A "poverty mentality" says, "I can't give anything. I only have enough for me," like the widow to whom Elijah was sent at Zarephath. (1 Kings 17:12.)

However, she *obeyed* the prophet and came out ahead in spite of that mentality.

The real cornerstone of the foundation for gaining wealth is *obedience*. However, I did not want to talk about that until I clearly proved *who* owns all the wealth, because *obedience* starts with tithing. There has been a lot of teaching today that those under the New Covenant do not give tithes. So, unless you see God owns it all, you will not see that He has a right to ask for tithes and offerings under the New Covenant as well as the Old.

The widow's obedience overrode her "poverty mentality." Many Christians and ministries could learn a lesson from her. All of those letters I get from ministries that "are about to go under" are placed in "File Z," the wastebasket. If I am not led by the Holy Spirit to give, then I do not give a dime. Trying to play on my sympathy, or put me on a guilt trip, does not work. God only blesses your giving when *He* has told you to give — like the widow.

God does not have any sad stories. God is not broke. I have found out, as I mentioned earlier, that when it is God's vision you are fulfilling, the provisions have already been made. I am not moved by ministries or people who are into self-pity because they are serving God and broke.

If what you have is not enough to meet your need, give it away as seed and trust God for more. I know from my own personal life and from our church progress that this principle works. Giving will bring a harvest, a return.

Why do you think God had that widow give her last piece of bread to the preacher? If God moves on you to give the little you have to one of His servants, be sure it is Him, then do it. You will not lose by it, and you will receive a great blessing. If you obey God, no matter how crazy it seems, you will be blessed.

In our church and ministry, we do not beg. If the finances are not there, we do not do anything else until they are.

The bottom line is *you do not own anything.* God owns the wealth, but He has said He will see that it gets into our hands if we let Him order and direct the way it is dispersed. God has a certain planned distribution system for His wealth, but if you walk contrary to His plan, you will not be distributing very long!

Ignorance also will close God's hand, which is why He is having me write this book. So those who read it will know the truth and will be able to lay a firm foundation for the receiving and distributing of wealth. God would not have put as much about wealth and how to handle riches in the Bible as He did, if He had not intended for His people to have wealth.

3
Stay in Line With the Word

In addition to learning how God has arranged for us to get wealth, we need to get His mind on how to handle wealth. Because He already is "wealthy," He knows how to *handle* it. You do not go to a person who has a hundred-dollar surplus and ask him how to make, invest, or properly spend a million dollars. He cannot tell you anything, because he has never been there.

The Bible is a road map and an owner's manual to tell us the direction to take and how to maintain the "vehicle" (body), also the "equipment" (soul — mind, will, and emotions). *You*, the inner man, are the real person who lives in the body and uses the equipment. However, only the Owner and Maker knows all of the potential governing His creation.

Suppose you start for California from somewhere in the eastern United States. If you get off-target even a little bit, you might end up in Baja California or Oregon. If you get off-line with the map a lot, you could end up in South America or Canada. Either way, you will miss your destination, plus whatever you were supposed to see and do along the way.

Your "journey" through life is no different. Therefore, it is important that you be "lined up" exactly with the target, which is God's purpose and plan for you.

On the other hand, if you do not maintain the body — exercise, balanced work and rest, and proper diet — your vehicle will wear out along the way. If you do not maintain the equipment, keeping your mind and emotions operating through the fruit of the Spirit (Gal. 5:22,23), your equipment will "malfunction" and possibly cause you to lose sight of the target.

Your *will* is the "direction finder." If your will is not set in agreement with God's will and under the authority of the Holy Spirit, you will wander off target. You might even turn around and go backwards!

You do not find your true direction in life through the world's thinking, and you do not find out how to handle finances God's way through what the world can teach you. The world's systems work opposite to God's in every situation. The spiritual way of handling money does not come from your senses, your flesh, or your mind. Spiritual money management comes out of your spirit. The Spirit of God gives *your spirit* revelation, wisdom, and understanding.

Did you ever make a deal that you wished you had not? If so, you did not seek the mind of Christ on the situation but went into it simply because it "looked good." Then, probably, about two months later, you were crying out to God about why He "let you get into it."

He "let" you, because you did not ask Him! However, if you had learned managing and receiving finances in line with the Word, you would have known ahead of time that something was wrong with that deal without even asking the Lord. His Word already would have told you.

The Word says we *have* the mind of Christ:

For who hath known the mind of the Lord, that he may instruct him? (Who can correct God?) **But we have the mind of Christ.**

1 Corinthians 2:16

John 15:15 records that Jesus told His disciples, at that point in His ministry, He could call them friends. The reason, He said, was because He had made known to them *all* the things He had heard of the Father. Therefore, in the gospels, you have "the mind of Christ" on every area of life or every situation you might encounter.

Also, in the rest of the New Testament, the apostles and authors expound on or expand what Jesus said. Jesus, in His turn, quoted extensively from "the Law and the Prophets" (the Old Testament) and spent time pointing out the difference between what the Old Testament writers *actually* and literally had said and what the scribes and Pharisees taught.

Every time Jesus said, "You have heard it said," the verses following that phrase straightened out some wrong beliefs or wrong teachings that were "traditions and doctrines of men." (Matt. 5:21,27,31,33,38,43.)

Therefore, through the written Word, we *have* the mind of Christ, which is the mind of God, on anything we need to know. When you are born again, the Holy Spirit comes to dwell within you, and His wisdom and revelation is the "mind of Christ in you." In addition, if you are filled with the Holy Spirit, you have another way of ascertaining God's mind, and that is through your prayer language.

If you are operating in the world's wisdom, through whatever source, you have a counterfeit wisdom. You do not have the real thing. Sooner or later, that wisdom will cause you to fall or to be defeated.

Seek Wisdom, Not Worldly Knowledge

In Proverbs 1:20-23, Wisdom says, "I was crying in the streets and in the gates, 'Oh, you simple one, don't make that deal!' But you were not listening. All you saw were dollar signs. All you saw was a 'get-rich-quick' scheme. When you seek me by meditating on the Word of God day and night, you will begin to deal successfully."

When the Scripture says, **Let the peace of God rule in your hearts** (Col. 3:15), that means, "Let the peace of God be the umpire, the decision maker."

If what you are about to get into does not carry a "peace" with it, that lack is the Spirit of God trying to let you know to "back off" that deal, whatever it is. If you have a slight uneasiness, a "feeling" that maybe something is wrong — in other words, a disquieting impression — usually that is the Holy Spirit witnessing to your spirit that something *is* wrong.

Many people have had this experience when contemplating marriage and ignored it because they were so in love. You need to go into these things slowly, taking time to seek a clear witness from God, then you will not have to repent at all.

Take your time, seek the Lord, meditate on scriptures that relate to whatever area of life this circumstance falls into. Be absolutely sure you have the mind of Christ on that situation and the peace of the Holy Spirit in your heart. Then you can be secure in asking God's blessings on it.

Look at some verses in Proverbs, and you will see that godly wisdom is stored up for the righteous.

For the Lord giveth wisdom: out of his mouth cometh knowledge and understanding.

He layeth up sound wisdom for the righteous: he is a buckler to them that walk uprightly.

When wisdom entereth into thine heart, and knowledge is pleasant unto thy soul;

Discretion shall preserve thee, understanding shall keep thee:

To deliver thee from the way of the evil man . . . .
Proverbs 2:6,7,10-12

If you look up all of the scriptures on wisdom, you will see that God says over and over that *wisdom* is more precious than any of the world's precious metals or other treasures. (Prov. 3:13,14.) Why is that? Wisdom is the most precious thing in the world because *wisdom* guards the path of the just and preserves the way of the saints. (Prov. 2:20.)

Wisdom (meaning the wisdom of Christ) makes sure you do not fall into any pits, get involved in any bad deals, or place yourself in a position where God's hand must be closed over your finances. God will make sure you lack nothing, if you first seek His wisdom.

Solomon, who was known as the "wisest man on earth," wrote:

Happy is the man that findeth wisdom, and the man that getteth understanding.

For the merchandise of it is better than the merchandise of silver, and the gain thereof than fine gold.

She (wisdom) is more precious than rubies: and all the things thou canst desire are not to be compared unto her.

Length of days is in her right hand; and in her left hand riches and honour.

Her ways are ways of pleasantness, and all her paths are peace.

**She is a tree of life to them that lay hold upon
her: and happy is every one that retaineth her.**
Proverbs 3:13-18

So the Lord is saying, ''Get hold of My wisdom,
but with that wisdom, get some understanding.''

All of God's attributes, except wisdom, are spoken
of in the masculine gender. However, wisdom is called
''she.'' God was trying to paint us a picture through
that use of feminine gender. He wanted us to see how
desirable wisdom is, to embrace and hold ''her'' and
keep her close to you.

Here is how you embrace wisdom: You embrace
the Word, study it, read it, and keep it close to you.
There are several scriptures about wisdom that really
will help you, if you meditate on them: Proverbs 8:1-5,
9:1-6,11, 10:13, 14:6,30, 16:16,23, 18:4, 19:8, 24:3-5.)

If you really get hold of wisdom, you will continue
to seek her and never be totally satisfied. The more
wisdom you have, the more you want. A ''satisfied''
Christian is a backslidden Christian, because in God,
there is no stopping place.

A Christian always is going forward or backward,
there is no ''maintenance'' mode.

There have been times when I have tackled things
with no knowledge at all of how to do them. But I
moved out in faith, and then the wisdom of God began
to flow. Potentially, we have the ability through the
mind of Christ to do whatever comes to our hands to
do. The Holy Spirit inside us is omniscient,
omnipotent, and omnipresent.

When I have a problem I cannot solve, I say,
''Holy Spirit, I need Your help now.'' And He helps
me out. He is my wisdom. First Corinthians 1:30 says
that Christ has been made unto us ''wisdom,
righteousness, sanctification, and redemption.''

If we are going to walk in the blessings of God and get and keep the wealth of God, then we need to find out how God did it. We need His wisdom to find out the plan He instituted in the earth to govern wealth. If you are willing to ask and keep on asking, you will receive, the Word says (Matt. 7:7), and that includes wisdom.

Do not "beg" God for things, He is your "daddy." Begging does not move God; *faith moves God.*

God Teaches Us To Profit

Isaiah 48:17 says that God is "the Lord, our Redeemer, the Holy One of Israel," and the One Who teaches us to profit. Perhaps you thought that by working twelve to sixteen hours a day, you would get wealthy. Instead, you have worn out your body, and still you are broke. You owe everyone in town, and you wonder, "How does the world do it?"

The world's principles are not for the Church. God has a plan for His Church that the world would envy. God's plan is opposite to the way the world thinks. His ways are not our ways; His thoughts are not our thoughts. (Isa. 55:8.)

The secret things belong to God, but those things that He has revealed belong to us. (Deut. 29:29.) There are certain things God has revealed in His Word about wealth that guarantee you will walk in so much blessing you cannot stand it.

If you want everything you do to prosper, *stay* in the Word. Meditate in the Bible, and you will gain wisdom, understanding, and knowledge. You will be "like a tree planted by water" (Ps. 1:3), and you will never want for anything. You will be so strong that nothing can move you.

Jesus said, "Those who are weary and heavy-laden, come to Me, and I'll give you rest." (Matt. 11:28.) If you are laboring, you need to go to Jesus, who will show you how to rest in His Word. He will show you how to walk in wealth and not struggle. You will have so much, the world will envy you.

Once you come to rest, then He will put His yoke on you and bring discipline to your life. After that, if you stay in the Word, He can show you how to profit. He dealt personally with me once I began to study His Word on finances. He spoke to me about some things, and I found many examples in the Bible of what He said.

For instance, the Holy Spirit once called me "a hypocrite."

He said, "Son, you get up in front of your people and say you do not have a building-fund drive. Yet, right there on your offering envelopes, 'Building Fund' is written in the middle. So even when no finances are needed for building, you continue to take up offerings for that. What if your church was completely finished? People would be giving into a fund for which there was no project."

I said, "Okay, Lord, You're right."

Then He showed me the example of Moses' building the tabernacle. The Holy Spirit showed me that, when Moses came before the people at the command of God, He had a plan, and when that plan was fulfilled, Moses stopped taking up a collection.

The Lord said to me, "When *I* call for an offering, I put a willing heart into the people, and there will not have to be a 'pull' by the leader. The people will only have to know that I have need of something.

"They will say, 'Oh, the Lord has need of this. Let's go home and get it and bring it back to Him.' " (Mark 14:12-16.)

Moses said, "I need this and this and this to build or to make this, this, and this."

The Word says the Israelite women went home and wove the linen. (Ex. 35:25.) Those who had gold and silver brought some. The people kept on bringing things until Moses had to stop them. (Ex. 36:6,7.) He did not have "building-fund drives" going year in and year out. There was a specific time when Moses needed contributions, and that time did not last seven or eight years. Some churches have been trying for years to raise funds to build. That is not how God does it. When He moves, He moves quickly.

There are times when God all of a sudden opens His hand over your house and drops wealth. Then the Holy Spirit will say, "Bring Me an offering for *My* house."

This area of not staying in line with the Word on raising finances is a source of trouble to many ministries. They either build things God did not say to build, or they do not wait for Him to bring in the provisions.

Ministers must be careful not to feel they must save the whole world by themselves. God always has other people who have parts to play in His plan. Never think you are the only one left, as Elijah did — until the Lord told him there were "seven thousand more who had not bowed down to Baal." (1 Kings 19:18.)

When you do your part, God has someone else to do other parts. Your part may be to disciple those who have been evangelized; your part may be to do the evangelizing; or your part may be to train others to do the work of the ministry. (Eph. 4:12.)

Some ministers get in trouble through stepping outside of their callings. If you are called to preach, that is where God's anointing will be. Then if you try to teach, there will be no anointing. Because you have stepped outside your call and are doing something God has not assigned you to do, you become open to errors or temptations of some kind.

When the Bible says that God "teaches us to profit," that is not referring only to money. God teaches us to profit in other ways as we listen. When the tabernacle was being constructed, God called two men named Bezaleel and Aholiab to make all of the artifacts. Then God taught those two men how to profit from their calling as craftsmen by giving them the wisdom to teach others. (Ex. 31:2-6.)

The rest of their lives, I am sure they taught apprentices craftsmanship and profited financially.

> **Then wrought Bezaleel and Aholiab,** *and every wise-hearted* **man, in whom the Lord had put wisdom and understanding to know how to work all manner of work for the service of the sanctuary, according to all that the Lord had commanded.**
>
> **Exodus 36:1**

When God was ready for His tabernacle to be constructed, He did not go to the Canaanites, the unsaved but skilled craftsmen, to get people with ability to do the work.

He said to them, and is saying to us, "See? You may think you have no ability at all, but when I get ready to do something, I will put wisdom in you to do it. I will equip you with skills that you never had before.''

In my own church, we have seen God bring in craftsmen or people skilled in certain kinds of work *before* we needed them. When He was ready for us to move into television, He provided the equipment. Already, there was someone in the church trained in that area. When we were ready to build, a born-again, Spirit-filled, Bible-totin' building contractor was already a member of the church.

God says, ''When I get ready for a project, it will be taken care of — and when I am ready for you to do your part — you will be able to do it.''

Your Part Is To Be Willing

Only those who are willing will receive the benefits and profit, however. When Bezaleel and Aholiab discovered they could make artifacts that brought a lot of money, what if they had not been willing to use those abilities for God? What if they had decided to go into business for themselves? What would have happened?

You might think God would have taken the abilities away from them, but you would be wrong. God's gifts and callings are irrevocable. (Rom. 11:29.) What those men lost would have been rewards in Heaven. One day before the Lord, they would have had to give an account of how they used His talents, how they fulfilled His call and purpose on their lives, and why they did not obey.

That is what the parable of the talents is all about. (Matt. 25:15-28.) Being unwilling to multiply for Him what God gives you makes you ''an unfaithful servant.'' Being gifted by God but unwilling to put your money or your abilities to work for Him can be a dangerous place to be. The only way for cash or abilities to increase is to *invest* them in good soil.

Ecclesiastes 11:1 says:

Cast thy bread upon the waters: for thou shalt find it after many days.

That does not mean the current is going to literally turn around and flow uphill in the natural. However, spiritual events are opposite to the world's. Solomon meant whatever you give out will come back to you — the "law of sowing and reaping," in other words.

In Philippians 4:15-20, Paul said to the Christians at Philippi, "No one got in on this set-up of giving and receiving into my need but you people. You invested at my request, and because of that, all your needs will be met according to God's riches in glory." (v. 19.)

That promise is not applicable to your life unless you do what the Philippians did to receive the promise. There is no such thing as promising to tithe *after* you make more money or giving more *after* you make more money. That will be a lost cause. God's kingdom does not work that way.

You must give in order to receive. Even for salvation, you "give" your heart in order to receive the life of God within you. If you plant, then you will receive the harvest, and you cannot plant stingily. That is where "willing" comes in. You must plant according to the harvest you want to receive, not according to what you have extra.

Most people want to give "Georges" (dollar bills, which have George Washington's likeness), and receive back "Mr. Hamiltons" or "Mr. Jacksons." There is one thing you can say about "George," however. He is faithful. Every time the church doors open, "George," is there. He shows up all of the time. You do not see nearly as much of the other two.

God looks for people to bless who have willing attitudes to give Him the part that is His — and more. The problem with most Christians today is that they believe everything they have is theirs — and they feel good about themselves when they "tip" God a little bit. The Church must learn that you cannot tip God and be blessed.

4

The Purpose of Wealth

When you get wealth, what are you going to do with it?

If you do not know the purpose of a thing, you may abuse it. You need to know the purpose of wealth in order not to misuse it after you are able to walk in the faith to receive it. You also need to know the purpose of wealth so that you can disburse it properly after you get it, thereby putting yourself in spiritual position to receive more.

There is a three-fold purpose for wealth in the Word of God:

1. In order for His covenant (vision, purpose, and plans) to be established in the earth. (Deut. 8:18.)

2. To have something to give to those who have legitimate needs. (Isa. 58:7-11.)

3. For your own enjoyment and blessing. (1 Tim. 6:17.)

I am going to deal with each of these in the order in which they are found in the Bible: first, for God; then, for others, and lastly, for self. That is the order of priorities for the use of wealth.

The first place we find someone being blessed with prosperity in the Word is in the narrative about Abraham and his lifestyle. The reason for Abraham being blessed was to establish the Covenant *and* to give to, or to bless, others.

God began to get Abraham into a position to be blessed when He called him out of his native land and told him to travel to a better place. The first thing God did was get Abram, as he was known to his family and native friends, away from familiar surroundings and away from his relatives.

Later, God changed his name to *Abraham*, "father of many nations," as a perpetual sign that His promises would come true. (Gen. 17:5.) When God changed Abram's name, he only had one son, and Ishmael was not by Abram's wife, Sarah, but by a maidservant. After the promised son, Isaac, Abraham had six more sons.

From those natural descendants come the Arabs, the Israelites (of whom the Jews are left today), and whatever peoples descended from the other six sons. In addition, there are those descendants of Abraham who are a spiritual nation. Indeed, as God said, a great multitude of peoples and more than one nation. (Gen. 48:19.)

Would these promises have come to pass if Abram had remained in his hometown among his relatives and those who had known him all of his life? I think not.

Would God want you to "get away from" your relatives? Unfortunately, in many cases, this is necessary for your spiritual growth — if not literally, then figuratively. We are told in the New Testament that even Jesus could do no mighty works in His hometown of Nazareth. In fact, Jesus is the one who said a prophet is without honor in his hometown. (Matt. 13:57,58.)

Jesus' neighbors said, "He can't be the Messiah. Don't we know His family? We know His parents, His brothers and sisters, and we saw Him grow up. If He grew up here among us, and we know His family, He could not possibly even be a prophet or anyone important." (Matt. 13:54-56.)

An old adage says that "familiarity breeds contempt." Somehow, when people have known you a long time, they are not able to get past the fact that they have placed you into a certain "pigeonhole." Few of your relatives will be able to see you differently than "good old Joe" or whatever other category in which they have always known you.

Most people who get a vision from God about how He wants them to be and what He wants them to do had better not tell it to their kinfolk! Many of them will "cut you down," thinking, if not actually saying, "What? God use *you*? No way."

Sometimes, they actively try to discourage you. They will feed doubt and disbelief into your mind — and with the best intentions, usually. They do not want you to "get hurt," to try something and fail, or to "get out of your class."

You have to get away from your close friends and relatives sometimes in order to hear God rightly. Even parents can hinder what God wants you to do and be by projecting their own ambitions and desires onto you. How many fathers want their sons to be football heroes because they were — or even because they were not? Many sons are expected to fulfill the dreams and visions of the fathers.

Please do not ever force *your* vision on your child. God made each of us an individual with a separate vision and plan for life. Let God bring to pass His vision for that child. Do not force your dream on your child. Let God fulfill His purpose in that life.

Trust God enough to be sure He does not make any mistakes.

God promised Abram if he would leave his familiar environment and set out on this trek into an unknown land, He would make of him a great nation and bless him abundantly personally, as well as make his name famous and distinguished. In addition, God told Abram he would be a blessing to others.

Giving To Fulfill God's Vision

The second place in the Bible where we find God blessing His people with wealth *to fulfill His vision, purpose, and plans in the earth* is in Exodus, where Abraham's natural descendants have expanded into the millions and have fallen into the bondage of slavery to a Pharoah "who did not know Joseph." (Ex. 1:8.)

In Exodus 35:4-9, you will find that God told Moses to ask the Israelites for a free-will offering in order to construct a tabernacle in which He could dwell while traveling with the people through the wilderness and into the Promised Land. And the Israelites brought gold, silver, precious jewels, and fine fabrics. (Ex. 36:21-29.)

Where did they get this wealth? They had been in slavery for years. If you read the account of the exodus, you will find that God told Moses to have them ask the Egyptians for presents when they left. (Ex. 11:2,3; 12:35,36.)

I have found from the Word that, when God gets ready to have someone build a building or develop a project for Him, He has blessed the people in advance so that they have it to give. God never had to initiate building-fund programs or fund-raising drives. This is a place I feel the Church is missing it today.

If pastors taught the principles of wealth, blessings, and God's will for His people to prosper, the people would have money to bring into the storehouse whenever God called for it.

Also, the Israelites did not have to use their wealth to supply their needs. *God* supplied their needs of food, water, and clothes (by supernaturally causing the clothes not to wear out). When God called for donations to build the tabernacle, the people had such willing hearts that God finally had to tell them through Moses to stop giving. (Ex. 36:3-7.)

When God begins to fulfill one of His visions, He already has the provisions in place.

The next place to look for this principle being implemented is when Israel was ready to build a temple, God's second dwelling place on earth. In Second Samuel 8:1-12, we see David winning gold shields in battle and bringing them into Jerusalem to store for the temple.

David exacted tribute of bronze from those he defeated, and others sent him gifts. When Solomon was ready to build the temple, much of what was needed already had been collected by David. (1 Chron. 29:2-9.)

Several hundred years later, the twelve tribes divided into two nations. Then the ten-tribed nation of Israel disappeared, divorced by God and "scattered" among the other nations of the world (Amos 9:9). And the two-tribed nation of Judah later went into exile but had a promise of return. After seventy years, God used Ezra, and then Nehemiah, to lead back into the Promised Land all of those who wanted to come out of Babylon.

When the remnant of fifty thousand returned, they had amassed wealth during their exile in Babylon enough to give toward the restoration of the temple. (Ezra 1:3-6.) God also used two Gentile kings to finance the rebuilding of His temple. (Ezra 5:13,14, 6:1-12.) Cyrus, king of Persia, first provided the supplies needed, then Darius, his successor completed the work. Cyrus also returned the treasures Nebuchadnezzar had taken out of the temple in Jerusalem. (Ezra 1:7-11, 5:13-15.)

In every instance that God wanted something done, He provided a way for His people to get the wealth to fulfill His vision. The Bible does not say we work *for* God but that we are laborers *with* Him. (1 Cor. 3:6.) At a certain point in His life, Jesus told the disciples they were no longer servants to Him but friends. (John 15:15.)

We are to fulfill God's purpose for mankind, *to have dominion* over the earth.

> **And God said, Let us make man in our image, after our likeness: and let them have dominion over the fish of the sea, and over the fowl of the air, and over the cattle, and over all the earth, and over every creeping thing that creepeth upon the earth.**
>
> **And God blessed them, and God said unto them, Be fruitful, and multiply, and replenish the earth, and subdue it: and have dominion over the fish of the sea, and over the fowl of the air, and over every living thing that moveth upon the earth.**
>
> **Genesis 1:26,28**

We are to subdue the world, and we have been voluntarily giving up our inheritance and letting the world subdue us. Too many generations of the Church have been "Esaus" and not "Josephs" or "Davids."

Solomon wrote that the wealth of the sinner is laid up for the just, and we need to begin to claim that promise. (Prov. 13:22.)

Wealth Is for Giving to Others

God always makes provision for the needy, whom Jesus said "are always with us." (Matt. 26:11.)

However, you are not a good steward of the money God gives you if you allow sentimentality and "do-goodism" to cloud your hearing God on how and to whom you are to give. There is a difference between "poor" and "lazy." Some people not only want others to take care of them, but they *expect* it. Many people feel they "have it coming" to them. That is called a "welfare mentality."

Aid to the poor was established by the government in the 1930s as part of President Franklin D. Roosevelt's New Deal programs. Until then, "charity," or aid to the jobless and otherwise needy, was provided by individuals, churches, and charitable organizations.

Today, there are many people who genuinely need to be helped and are grateful for the nation's collective generosity. However, there are others who are simply "plain lazy," who have grown up expecting the government to provide for their needs.

The Bible says if you will not work, you are not supposed to eat! (2 Thess. 3:10.)

In all of your giving, you need to be led by the Holy Spirit. Sometimes you can get in the way of God's dealing with people by giving at the wrong time and to the wrong ones. Part of the purpose of wealth is to minister to those who, for some legitimate reason, cannot help themselves.

If people are really in need, they should be helped. But they also need to be taught how to get out of that need and how to prosper so that they can have finances to give to the Lord and to others. We need to teach in our churches that God is our source, not some man-made organization.

Christians need to learn how to live by the economic system of Heaven, apart from man's systems, and pastors need to teach their sheep to live by God's economic principles.

Proverbs 19:17 says that the person who has pity on the poor is lending money to the Lord, and the Lord will repay it. Do you believe God pays His debts? If you do, then expect to receive back what you have given to the poor. Do not expect it back from the one to whom you give. Expect it back from the Lord, in order to have some to give to someone else.

Proverbs 22:9 says the person who gives bread to the poor will be blessed. That person is said to have *a bountiful eye,* a mindset toward giving. That means "a generous, giving eye."

Proverbs 28:27 says the one who gives to the poor will not be in want himself. But the person who "hides his eyes" from the needs of the poor will have many a curse! There is never one side to God's promises. There always is a consequence if you abide by them and a consequence if you do not.

There is no middle ground for God's people where you can simply ignore the principles and commandments and think you are as safe as if you abided by them. Jesus said if you were not *for* Him, you were *against* Him. (Matt. 12:30.) So your own lack could be tied to not operating in God's instructions concerning giving.

I do not like the consequences of not obeying, which we call ''curses.'' Jesus said in His Sermon on the Mount to keep giving to him who keeps begging from you and not to turn away from him who would borrow at interest. (Matt. 5:42.) Notice he did not say for you to borrow. You are supposed to be the head and not the tail, remember?

Under the Old Covenant, an Israelite was to be forgiven any debts every seven years and not to be taken to court to collect it. However, that only applied to those under the covenant. Those outside the covenant were not forgiven debts and could be taken to court to collect. (Deut. 15:1-3.)

In our day, that principle translates to Christians, Abraham's descendants under the New Covenant. (Gal. 3:7,29.) That means you are not supposed to take a brother or sister in the Lord to court. The Lord was saying it was better to suffer the loss, chalk it up to experience, and forget it.

Abraham's blessings continued down to Isaac and on to Jacob. The family blessing usually was included with the ''birthright.'' The oldest son was to get the blessing and inherit the birthright of becoming the next patriarch and head of the family. However, we are given pattern after pattern in the Word where God overturned this law of inheritance and gave the blessings and birthright to a younger son.

God said He also would bless Ishmael, Abraham's oldest son, but *Isaac* was to have the birthright. (Gen. 17:19-21.) Isaac's oldest son, Esau, sold his birthright to the younger son, Jacob, but Jacob stole the blessing in addition. However, God had prophesied this turn of events when the twins were born. (Gen. 25:23.)

Then Jacob had twelve sons, with Reuben being the oldest. Because of some sins, he lost both blessing and birthright. (Gen. 49:3,4.) Jacob gave the birthright to the fourth son, Judah, and the blessing to Joseph's sons, Ephraim and Manasseh. Joseph was not even the second son, but the eleventh. And Jacob gave Joseph's younger son the greater blessing. (Gen. 48:17-20.)

Solomon got birthright, right to reign, and the blessings. And he was David's youngest son. Why? God was painting us a picture:

*He owns all the wealth, and He is the one who disposes of things according to His will and purpose. (Prov. 16:33.)

*Adam was God's first man, but he lost his birthright and blessing, and God gave them to His "last" man, Jesus (1 Cor. 15:45) — who was not created but "the firstborn." (Col. 1:15,18.) All of those second sons who received the inheritance of their fathers pointed us to Jesus.

And, the Word of God says that we are "joint-heirs" with Jesus! Therefore we have the right to the blessings of Abraham and of God. We are the inheritors of the birthright and the blessing along with Jesus. What He received for Himself, He shares with us.

> **The Spirit itself beareth witness with our spirit, that we are the children of God:**
>
> **And if children, then heirs; heirs of God, and *joint-heirs* with Christ; if so be that we suffer with him, that we may be also glorified together.**
>
> **Romans 8:16,17**

From this you ought to be able to clearly see that if you do not set yourself in expectancy to receive the blessings, you are walking away from something that is already yours.

Blessings are given to you when you become born again, and if you do not choose to receive them, you become like Esau. You have counted your birthright of such little value that you have traded it for a "mess of the world's pottage." (Gen. 25:34.) Like Esau, you may one day repent with much bitterness and tears, as Hebrews 12:17 says:

> **For ye know how that afterward, when he would have inherited the blessing, he was rejected: for he found no place of repentance, though he sought it carefully with tears.**

Wealth Is for You To Enjoy

The third purpose for wealth is to enjoy. When you begin walking in wealth, and religious people try to tell you that you should not be enjoying the "good life" — and, in fact, should not even have it — you need some scripture to give them. Try 1 Timothy 6:17-19:

> **Charge them that are rich in this world, that they be not high-minded, nor trust in uncertain riches, but in the living God, *who giveth us richly all things to enjoy*.**
>
> **That they do good, that they be rich in good works, ready to distribute, willing to communicate;**
>
> **Laying up in store for themselves a good foundation against the time to come, that they may lay hold on eternal life.**

Tell them everything God gives us is for us *to enjoy*. However, the best way is to follow the instructions in the rest of that chapter. Paul wrote that wealth first of all should be used to fulfill the first two parts of the Biblical purpose for wealth: financing

God's plans and visions and giving to those with legitimate needs.

Ecclesiastes 3:12,13 says there is nothing better than to do good in this life (for which you must have the finances), also that every man should enjoy the good of his labor, which is a gift from God.

> Wherefore I perceive that there is nothing better, than that a man should rejoice in his own works; for that is his portion: for who shall bring him to see what shall be after him?
>
> Behold that which I have seen: it is good and comely for one to eat and to drink, and to enjoy the good of all his labour that he taketh under the sun all the days of his life, which God giveth him: for it is his portion.
>
> Every man also to whom God hath given riches and wealth, and hath given him power to eat thereof, and to take his portion, and to rejoice in his labour; this is the gift of God.
>
> Ecclesiastes 3:22; 5:18,19

I wrote in the introduction to this book that we should ask first for wisdom, then riches and honor will follow. Proverbs 3:16 says exactly that:

> Length of days is in her right hand; and in her left hand riches and honour.

The word *honor* means glory and fame. That is our promise from God that if we seek His wisdom, He will bless us with long life and wealth. Then everyone will know about us.

5
The Cornerstone Is Tithing

The cornerstone of your blessings is tied up in one act of obedience, and *it is tithing*. Only eighteen to twenty percent of people who call themselves Christians in this country give tithes. That is the reason the entire Church has so much trouble with finances.

There is no scripture to back up the idea that we can withhold from the Lord what He asks for and still be blessed. All of the scriptures I find say that, when you do not tithe, you place yourself under a curse.

For those who say tithing is "under the law" and not for today, I remind you that tithing started with Abraham, more than four hundred years before God gave Israel the law through Moses. The promise of blessings and abundance was given to Abraham *before the law.*

When Israel became large enough to be counted in the millions, God gave Moses in detail His principles, commandments, and the consequences of not keeping their covenant responsibilities. Those consequences are the opposite of blessings, and they are called curses.

The first time *tithes* is mentioned in the Bible is with Abraham.

> And Melchizedek king of Salem brought forth bread and wine: and he was the priest of the most high God.
>
> And he blessed him, and said, Blessed be Abram of the most high God, possessor of heaven and earth:
>
> And blessed be the most high God, which hath delivered thine enemies into thy hand. And he (Abraham) **gave him** (Melchizedek, priest of the most high God and king of Salem) **tithes of all.**
>
> **Genesis 14:18-20**

Abraham then gave all the spoils back to the five kings, minus *ten percent!* And he did not keep any of what was taken for himself. (Gen. 14:21-24.)

Israel was instructed on giving the tithe all through Leviticus, Numbers, and Deuteronomy. In First and Second Chronicles you find mention of tithes being given, and in Nehemiah 10:38, 12:44, and 13:5, you see the Jews who returned from Babylon reinstituting the tithe.

The prophets Amos and Malachi, however, gave the strongest pictures of what happens to a child of God who does not give God what He counts as His out of what He gives you. In Amos 4:1-5, the Lord cited a list of things that showed Israel's rebellion and idolatry, and not giving tithes but every three years was one of them.

In Malachi, the Lord spelled out the consequences of not giving tithes:

> Will a man rob God? Yet ye have robbed me. But ye say, Wherein have we robbed thee? In tithes and offerings.
>
> Ye are cursed with a curse: for ye have robbed me, even this whole nation.
>
> Bring ye all the tithes into the storehouse, that there may be meat in mine house, and prove me now herewith, saith the Lord of hosts, if I will not open

**you the windows of heaven, and pour you out a
blessing, that there shall not be room enough to
receive it.**

**And I will rebuke the devourer for your sakes,
and he shall not destroy the fruits of your ground;
neither shall your vine cast her fruit before the time
in the field, saith the Lord of hosts.**

**And all nations shall call you blessed: for ye shall
be a delightsome land, saith the Lord of hosts.**

Malachi 3:8-12

It cannot be any plainer that God counts only ten
percent of what His children have as His, although
literally, He owns it all. It also could not be any plainer
that not giving tithes is robbing God. Robbing God
closes His hand to you and opens the way for the
devourer to destroy the fruits of whatever you do.

Your success in school, on the job, and at home;
your walking in divine health, and your financial
blessings are all tied up with the tithe. You either tithe,
or you always live a life of defeat, always wondering
why your "bucket has a hole in it."

Haggai explained why this happens:

**Ye have sown much, and bring in little; ye eat,
but ye have not enough; ye drink, but ye are not filled
with drink; ye clothe you, but there is none warm;
and he that earneth wages earneth wages to put it into
a bag with holes.**

Thus saith the Lord of hosts; Consider your ways.

Haggai 1:6,7

The Lord was talking to them about not bringing
into His house what they were supposed to; therefore,
the devourer was destroying their crops and stealing
their blessings.

Tithing Has Never Been Changed

You may be one of those who think tithing is not

for us today, but I can show you it is. In the first place, restoring to God ten percent is a law in the earth, and God never rescinds any of His laws. If He were going to rescind a law or principle, He would have rescinded the law of death over Adam and Eve.

Instead, God waited hundreds of years for a man to be born with whom He could cut a covenant. He cut covenant with Abraham to give Himself a right to send His Son to pay the penalty for Adam and Eve and any of their descendants who would receive it. If it were possible for God to change His character and laws, *that* is the one He would have changed.

Once God has set something in motion, it never changes, because He does not change. (Heb. 13:8.) In Malachi 3:6, God said, **For I am the Lord, I change not.**

In that particular context, God was speaking of His mercy. He was saying, ''You sons of Jacob, you never have been obedient the way you ought to have been. Although you deserve to be consumed because of your rebellion and disobedience, you have not been because *I do not change.*''

God said, ''I made a covenant with your father Abraham, therefore I will honor that. In later years, I am going to send you someone to turn the hearts of the fathers to the children, and vice versa, **lest I come and smite the earth with a curse** (Mal. 4:6).''

However, God was saying also, ''I do not change in any way, manner, or attitude. *I do not change ever.*''

God said to Israel, and He is saying to us today, ''You had better be glad I don't change! Because, if I did change, I would have to wipe you out.''

As much as Christians ''mess up'' today, and have down through the years, if God changed, He would have "pulled the plug" on us. However, simply because He *does* not change, there will come those times when judgment cannot be withheld any longer — or He would have changed as far as His justice is concerned.

He always says, "Return to me, and I will return to you."

In our generation, we had better think seriously about returning to Him in all our ways. Most people quote the blessings of Leviticus 26 and Deuteronomy 28, but believe the rest of those chapters — the curses — "are not for us today." You cannot separate covenant clauses like that. If the blessings of Abraham are for us when we obey (Gal. 3), then it should be obvious that not obeying opens us up to the curses.

It is not according to any laws — even those governing nature — to have one side of them true but not the other. That would be the same as saying:

Because of the law of gravity, we are able to live and walk around on the surface of the earth without flying off into space. However, the "curse" or consequence of ignoring that law is not for us today. We can jump off a cliff and not break bones or even die when we land. We are not under those "old laws," we are under the New Covenant which only has blessings.

That is a one-sided doctrine that goes against every pattern and example we are given in Scripture. David was one of the most godly men in the Bible. He followed after God's own heart to do His will (Acts 13:22), yet when he disobeyed God's moral laws, he certainly came under a curse! (2 Sam. 12:14.)

If you want a New Testament example, look at Ananias and Sapphira. (Acts 5:1-11.) They kept something that had been promised to God, and the consequences were about as severe as they could be. They did not have to promise God the proceeds from the piece of land, but they did voluntarily, with no coercion.

They could have come back to the apostles, repented of that vow, and said, ''We have decided we can't do this. Will you forgive us?'' In that case, the penalty would not have fallen on them. But they lied to the Holy Spirit about giving, lied to Peter, and broke a vow to God.

From the time you came into the knowledge that tithing is from God and still chose not to tithe, you owe God those back tithes. Some Christians' debts to the Lord are in the millions. But I have good news. You can repent, cancel the debt today, and begin to walk in obedience. Then your life will turn around, and you will begin to be victorious. God's hand will be opened to you again.

God's Laws Are Part of Him

God's law of giving applies to everything He does as well as to what we do. He gave *one* Son and received back billions of us. Abraham was willing to give one son to God as a sacrifice, and God allowed him to substitute a ram. Then Abraham gained in return billions of natural and spiritual children.

You must understand that it is not the money involved that matters so much, *it is the obedience.* Abraham obeyed God, and the promises came true. Adam and Eve disobeyed and lost everything for them and for their descendants.

In addition to God never changing His principles and laws, we see that Abraham was tithing into a priesthood that had no beginning or end. Jesus' priesthood came from that line. (Heb. 7:15-22.) It is of God and is to last throughout eternity.

In the first place, tithing is not based on the laws given to Israel. Those laws simply confirmed a heavenly law that already existed.

The tithe is tied up with everything you do. When you are not tithing, and you think you are getting some extra money — you do not get it. Something breaks, or the kids get sick, or something takes it.

When people begin to prosper, many times they forget about God. They think they will get a bigger car, a bigger house, and "catch God on the way back." You had better catch God on the way up, or you will be coming back down sooner than you think!

Deuteronomy says the proper procedure is to bring your tithe to the "priest" that is in your day. When you bring tithes to the church which you attend, you are bringing it to the "priest" of your day. Jesus is our high priest, but the five-fold offices are His representatives today.

There also are those who say, "I don't want some preacher getting all my tithe. I want to decide what happens to it."

Our precedent, or example, or pattern to follow, is the Old Testament way of handling tithes and offerings, which extended well into New Testament days. The priests determined how the tithes and offerings were divided.

The priests themselves were to get the best of what was given. (Lev. 7:34.) Why was that? They deserved the best *because they were standing in for God.* They represented the Lord of all creation. God has a certain order that He operates through.

If you do not follow God's order, His laws and principles will not work. Your blessings are tied up with how you treat and feel toward your pastor — that is, if you are in the right church and under the pastor that God has set you under.

God was saying, "If you do your part towards My priest, I will make sure you have no need. The tithes and offerings are supposed to take care of those who speak to you on My behalf."

One purpose of tithes and offerings is to make sure God's men and women in the fivefold offices are taken care of, because they sow into the people spiritual things. In return, God wants them to reap material things from the people.

You should not only tithe but teach your children to tithe. In Genesis, we come to Abraham's grandson, Jacob, who also lived about four hundred years before "the law" was handed down to Israel. Yet Jacob vowed to God that he would give him a tenth of all of the increase of his possessions. (Gen. 28:11.)

He was aware of tithe-giving, for he knew that his giving a tenth to God would mean God would be with him, supply his needs, protection, and clothes to wear.

Exodus 23:19 and Leviticus 27:30 say that all the tithe, whether it was crops or money, is the Lord's. *It was to be holy to the Lord.*

Jesus said specifically that He did not come to *do away* with the Law, but to fulfill it. (Matt. 5:17.) That means "complete" it, "make it perfect," write it on our hearts (Rom. 2:15) so that, with the help of the

Holy Spirit, we can walk in the righteousness to which the Law only pointed the way.

He corrected the scribes and Pharisees for legalism in giving tithes. He did not correct them *because* they gave tithes, but for thinking that giving tithes would make up for wrong attitudes and cover the breaking of other commandments.

> **Woe unto you, scribes and Pharisees, hypocrites! for ye pay tithe of mint and anise and cummin, and have omitted the weightier matters of the law, judgment, mercy, and faith: these ought ye to have done, *and not to leave the other undone.***
> **Matthew 23:23**

As we go on in this book, you will see that being obedient with the tithe is the cornerstone of your foundation for finances. However, it is not the only thing involved. Giving tithes is not an excuse for committing adultery, stealing, or even coveting. Because you keep one law of God does not mean you are excused for breaking the others.

But you notice Jesus said they *ought* to have given tithes. The other place in the New Testament where tithes are discussed is in Hebrews 7. This epistle is thought to have been written about thirty years after Jesus was caught up into Heaven.

The subject of the entire chapter is the priesthood of Jesus, said to be **an high priest for ever after the order of Melchisedec** (Heb. 6:20). The author of Hebrews was pointing out the difference between the natural order of priesthood, which followed the line of Levi, son of Jacob, and was a "picture" or forerunner of the *real* eternal priesthood, which was of an entirely different order.

The author pointed out that Abraham gave tithes long before the law was instituted. As a matter of fact, because the founder of the natural priesthood was in Abraham's loins at the time, Levi actually was considered to have given tithes to Melchizedek, of whose order Jesus is. (Heb. 7:10,11.)

Then the author of Hebrews says:

> **And here men that die receive tithes; but *there* he (Jesus) receiveth them, of whom it is witnessed that he liveth.**
>
> **Hebrews 7:8**

That is about as plain as it can be. The temple was still in existence when this book was written, and Levitical priests were still receiving tithes from Jews as part of the "old order" of things. The natural priesthood, sacrifices, and so forth that were a picture of Jesus, the true Promised Seed of Abraham, had been allowed a forty-year period of mercy before being destroyed in 70 A.D., the fulfillment of Jesus' prophesy against Jerusalem. (Matt. 24:1,2.)

However, just as plainly as the writer of Hebrews said natural priests were receiving tithes, he wrote that *Jesus* was receiving tithes *there*, by which he meant Heaven. If the disciples and the early Church gave tithes, knowing they were given to Jesus, the true High Priest, of whom Aaron and his sons were pictures, then where does it say that we do not have to do so as well?

Jesus, our High Priest and Mediator, hears our prayers in Heaven and answers. He receives our tithes in Heaven, although they are given to His representatives on earth. Then God opens His hand to those who are obedient.

So do not let anyone tell you tithing is not in the New Testament! A tenth of our increase always has been God's and always will be, as long as we are in a material universe.

Another problem with not giving tithes is that those who do also have to cope with some of the consequences of those who do not.

Sins of the Members Affect the Whole Body

Such a large percentage of the Church today rob God of His rightful percentage that it causes the majority of Christians to live under His closed hand. Also, their sin — and not giving tithe *is* a sin — affects the corporate Body. Not tithing is a sin because it is disobedience.

Disobedience carries a consequence with it that the Old Testament called a "curse." Disobedience is "covenant breaking," whether it is the Old Covenant or the New Covenant.

> But if ye will not hearken unto me, and will not do all these commandments;
>
> And if ye shall despise my statutes, or if your soul abhor my judgments, so that ye will not do all my commandments, but that ye *break my covenant*.
> Leviticus 26:14,15

Then God listed the curses that would follow, and said:

> And I will break the pride of your power; and I will make your heaven as iron, and your earth as brass:
>
> And your strength shall be spent in vain: for your land shall not yield her increase, neither shall the trees of the land yield their fruits.
> Leviticus 26:19,20

Again, our "pattern" is Israel. The Apostle Paul said all of those things in the Old Testament were written down as examples for us. (1 Cor. 10:11.)

When the Israelites entered the Promised Land under Joshua, God had already told them to kill everything that breathed in the cities of their inheritance. However, in peripheral cities, towns, and villages that would not make peace with them, they were to kill only the men. They were to save the women and children. And the Israelites could have the spoils, the cattle, and so forth of those places. He even gave instructions about which trees to cut. (Deut. 20:10-20.)

Of course, Israel had known for the past forty years to bring a tenth of those spoils into the tabernacle. Now, God said all the spoils of the first encounter with the Canaanites at Jericho (the firstfruits of their conquering the land) also belonged to Him.

But one man decided to keep some things from the victory at Jericho that belonged to God. He stole from God, and the whole nation was in trouble.

> **And they burnt the city with fire, and all that was therein: only the silver, and the gold, and the vessels of brass and of iron, they put into the treasury of the house of the Lord.**
>
> **Joshua 6:24**

> **But *the children of Israel* committed a trespass in the accursed thing: for Achan, the son of Carmi, the son of Zabdi, the son of Zerah, of the tribe of Judah, took of the accursed thing: and the anger of the Lord was kindled against the children of Israel.**
>
> **Joshua 7:1**

Achan stole some of the things meant for the tabernacle, some of the firstfruits offering, and hid them in his tent. (Josh. 7:20,21.) However, the Bible says *the children of Israel* committed the sin, although the rest of the Israelites knew nothing about what Achan had done.

The Body of Christ has a *better* covenant than Israel did. (Heb. 8:6.) So, if what one of them did affected the others and was seen by God as the sin of the entire body, how much more the sins of those in the Church? It is no wonder this country has fallen into inflation/depression so often during this century.

Since World War I, the trend has been away from keeping the principles and commandments of God, even in the Church. We are to be the "light" of the world. As the Church goes, so goes the community, the state, and the nation. God's mercy has overshadowed our finances because of the remnant, the twenty percent, that do tithe.

However, unless we repent and turn from our disobedient ways in tithes and merchandising the gifts of God, committing and condoning carnal sins, and acting as if we have no responsibility in our country's affairs, I am not sure how much longer His mercy will cover us.

If you doubt that God sees His Church as a whole or that what one does affects the rest, look at the picture Paul painted of the Church:

> For by one Spirit are we all baptized into one body, whether we be Jews or Gentiles, whether we be bond or free; and have been all made to drink into one Spirit.
>
> For the body is not one member, but many.
>
> If the foot shall say, Because I am not the hand, I am not of the body; is it therefore not of the body?
>
> And if the ear shall say, Because I am not the eye, I am not of the body; is it therefore not of the body?
>
> If the whole body were an eye, where were the hearing? If the whole were hearing, where were the smelling?

> But now hath God set the members every one of them in the body, as it hath pleased him.
>
> And if they were all one member, where were the body?
>
> But now are they many members, yet but one body.
>
> And whether one member suffer, all the members suffer with it; or one member be honoured, all the members rejoice with it.
>
> 1 Corinthians 12:13-20,26

Can you say because you stole something that only your hand sinned? Or because your foot walked in the wrong way that only your foot sinned? Or because your eyes lusted after something, only your eyes sinned?

No, you know that is not true. When you sin, your whole body is involved, and that is the way it is with the Body of Christ. Instead of judging and "pointing the finger" at those who fall, we need to repent on their behalf. We need to repent for the corporate Body. We need to stand in the gap, as Daniel did for Judah in Babylon. (Dan. 9:1-19.)

Daniel had not sinned personally, yet he repented for the whole body of Jews *as if it were his personal sin.*

Concerning Achan, it is written that he stole from God because he first *coveted* the beautiful Babylonian garment, the two hundred shekels of silver, and the fifty-shekel wedge of gold. (Josh. 7:21.) He was tempted first through lust of the eyes.

You may think you would never do that, and you probably would not lust enough for beautiful things you saw in some church to steal them. However, what about lusting after new clothes, or a new car, or even a dinner out with a movie enough to cause you to covet that ten percent of your week's pay set aside for God?

God said that because Achan partook of the thing set aside for God, he became a curse, and those things were accursed as well. When you take the tithe and use it for something else, that thing you bought becomes a curse, and you become cursed with it.

Some Christians drive fine cars and wear designer clothes bought with the tithe. Some even have the tithe wrapped around their wrists. They have counted God's money as their own. Those things bought with the tithe will not be blessed but cursed. They will be stolen, destroyed, or at least, leave the person with a lack of satisfaction with them.

6

You Cannot Tip God

The Word of God says that "he who sows sparingly will reap sparingly." (2 Cor. 9:6.) Another way of saying it is: **With the same measure that ye mete withal it shall be measured to you again** (Luke 6:38.) If your attitude is not right, and you are not really willing to give, you will give only a little. Then you probably will be upset when you get only a little back.

You planted one grain of corn but expect a yield of five acres. What it boils down to is that *you are trying to tip God*. You are giving a "token" offering but expecting an abundant yield. If the widow who gave the "mite" in the temple had given that penny out of several thousand dollars, Jesus would not have been so moved by her faith, her generosity, and love of God. (Luke 21:1-4.)

A good farmer goes out, looks at his fields, and says, "Plant all of it." He invests in seed for a harvest that he does not yet see. However, he knows the laws that govern sowing and reaping (Gal. 6:9,10), and he expects a yield based on how much he has planted. He will go in debt to buy the seed if need be.

What farmer have you ever heard of who plants seed and does not expect a harvest? In Genesis 8:22, the Bible says "seedtime and harvest" will remain as long as the earth lasts. That is not just talking about natural crops. That is talking about sowing and reaping in any area.

What is *your* attitude when you go to church, and it is time for the offering to be received? Giving offerings is required (Mal. 3:8), also all of God's children are supposed to give tithes, to give God the percentage for which He asked.

However, when it comes to offerings, please *do not tip God.* It will not do you or Him any good. Look at Exodus 35:4,5:

> **And Moses spake unto all the congregation of the children of Israel, saying, This is the thing which *the Lord commanded,* saying,**
>
> **Take ye from among you an offering unto the Lord: whosoever is of *a willing heart,* let him bring it, an offering of the Lord; gold, and silver, and brass.**

Notice, the Lord said *whoever is of a willing heart.* Does that deal with attitude? This passage is not talking about tithe, but about an offering *unto the Lord.* And God was saying that, if you are not willing to give to Him, do not give. *Offerings must be given freely and willingly,* or they are not ''good seed.''

You cannot have the attitude of ''tipping God'' a little bit today, but neither can you have the attitude of duty, being forced or coerced, or giving religiously (keeping the law for the sake of self-righteousness). In order to reap, you must plant willingly, gladly, and abundantly.

Do not let anyone else, in or out of the pulpit, put a ''guilt trip'' on you so that you give out of guilt, pressure, or feeling sorry for someone whose ministry is not going to make it if you do not give. That is not true compassion.

Give only when and to whom the Lord says, shows you, or gives you a witness.

He has said, as I have shown you in several different contexts, that *He* will call on those whom He wants to give. Then if they give with a willing heart, they will receive — in proportion to what they have given.

It is all right to plan for tomorrow, but God needs the cash today. There is nothing wrong with retirement funds, insurances, and savings accounts — as long as you give God His percentage and are ready to make whatever offerings He asks you for when He asks.

Over and above that, all of your finances should be available to God, if He asks for them. If He asks for your retirement fund, savings, or insurance policies: Be ready to give them to Him *willingly.* After all, they really belong to Him. You only are allowed the use of them.

The key to a good harvest is to be willing and generous. You cannot love someone without wanting to give things to them. Therefore, if you *truly* love God, you will have a desire to give to Him (into His works) whenever He asks.

People who love God and want to give usually are like the widow. They give a lot compared to what they have.

In 1990, my wife and I were confronted with the option of tithing or paying our bills. We opted to tithe. Not only that, but we were giving twenty percent of our income. The devil fought us tooth and nail for an entire year. We had bills running two and three months behind! It got so we did not want to even hear the phone ring — much less pick it up.

If you get in this position, let me remind you of something: When bill collectors call, *it is not their fault.* Remember *you* owe it, so watch your attitude, and do not get angry at them. The tendency is to feel they are "picking on" you or harassing you unjustly, and then you can feel justified in being angry or "bad mouthing" them back. That will only compound your spiritual problem and will not help the natural situation at all.

Some people get "unholy" quickly in a situation like this and even "cuss out" those who call. The first solution usually, when people begin not to be able to pay bills, is to get money on credit cards.

My wife and I did not do that. We went "snip, snip, snip" to our cards. We only kept one for emergencies, and that one has to be paid every thirty days. Basically, it is not a "credit" card. We closed every account we could, and for a whole year lagged behind. Not one time did we ever option not to give tithes and offerings.

If we had held back our tithes and offerings, we would have had no problem paying our bills. But from the Word of God, we knew that would simply make a hole for the devil to attack us even worse, and we would have no prospect of ever getting out of the mess.

We chose to believe and "prove" that God is our Source. Then January rolled around, and God showed us how to adjust one little thing. We made that small adjustment in organizing our lives, and every bill came current.

During that entire year of famine, not one time did a thought come to us about holding our tithes to pay a bill. The thought never really crossed our minds. I would rather take a chance on God, because if I had taken tithe to pay this month's bills, next month I would have had two to pay. That is not wisdom.

Giving Must Become a Way of Life

When you give tithes, the enemy will make sure enough stuff is coming at you so that you have every excuse not to give it. The sooner you learn that *you cannot afford not to,* the quicker you will get out of debt.

When God begins something in you, it is not just for a moment. Giving develops progressively into a lifestyle, once you become willing to operate in what God is putting in your heart. You do not become a generous giver today and go back tomorrow to being stingy. Although some people might be moved temporarily by circumstances — or a cause in which they have an interest — to give a large sum once. Then, after that, they would return to giving small amounts.

However, that would mean they were not "generous" or "cheerful givers," whose hearts were being changed toward God. That would show they had another motive for giving that large sum: Special interests, a liking for the person, church, or group to whom they gave the large sum, a desire to be liked or applauded, or even pride. ("*My* church must be the largest building in town," and so forth.)

Look again at the pattern the Lord gave us for offerings: Moses' building of the tabernacle.

> And they came, *every one whose heart stirred him up,* and *every one whom his spirit made willing,* and they brought the Lord's offering to the work of the tabernacle of the congregation, and for all his service, and for the holy garments.
>
> **Exodus 35:21**

Those who came were the ones whom the Spirit had dealt with in their hearts about giving. Later verses tell us that they not only gave *but* kept giving, until they had to be stopped. When God begins something, it is not simply for the moment.

Something is wrong with the Church's attitude toward giving to God today, the same thing that was wrong with the "rich, young ruler." *Most Christians do not have willing hearts to give.* They have not made giving a lifestyle, and their shepherds have not taught them to do so. If we are the children of God, why are we not able to live like He lives — out of debt? It is because of wrong attitudes of heart.

We have chosen to take the path of the world, to use the world's economic systems. But God's system is much higher than the world's. In the natural, it seems ludicrous to say that the key to receiving is to give away everything.

Was Jesus trying to impoverish that rich, young man? Was He trying to get him to give away everything and walk around begging? No, of course not. Jesus was trying to *help* him. There was no way he could lose. If he gave to the poor, He gave to God, who said He would repay. (Prov. 19:17.) If he gave offerings to the Lord, he would receive a harvest. If he gave up everything for Jesus, he would have received everything Jesus had in return.

God wants His people to come to the realization that the essence of receiving is giving. He wants us to understand that we do not have to prostitute ourselves to make money in order to have money. We can keep integrity. We do not have to sacrifice integrity for money.

Isaiah 32:8 says a "liberal" person looks for ways to be liberal. Another definition for the Hebrew word translated "liberal" is "noble." A noble person is one who is upright, generous, and who carries himself in a manner of dignity and integrity. God does not want us to compromise integrity to earn a living or make money. He wants us to be "noble," to be liberal-minded people.

Another verse Christians misinterpret is Acts 20:35, **It is more blessed to give than to receive.**

That does not mean the "Christian" principle is to give and never expect to receive. If you do not expect to receive — you will not receive!

Those who say, in such religious tones, "Oh, I don't want anything back. I just want to be a cheerful giver," will not get anything back. Basically, that is a prideful attitude, not Christ-like at all. Jesus expected a return on everything He did: giving His life to get billions of lives in return; giving up His heavenly glory and wealth to become King of kings and Lord of lords of the earth as well; and so forth. Everything He gave up, He knew would be returned one hundredfold. (Luke 8:8.)

There is one more thing to get straight in order to not "tip" God but to give Him what already is His and what He asks for in order for *you* to have seed to sow. That is: How do you figure the tithe?

I ask every audience the same question, "When you get your check, do you make all of it available to God, or have you paid the bills first?"

Do you go before God and say, "I thank You for the provisions, for the job You blessed me with to have this check. Lord, I give this check back to You. Any part You want or need, here it is. What do You want me to do with it?"

If God says, "Go on and pay your bills," then pay your bills.

Or, do you have the checks already written out and try to beat them to the bank?

God does not want us working just to pay bills. He wants us working in order to have something to give to someone else. If you do it God's way, you will not have the bills. Some folks work simply to pay bills. That is a small vision. That is finite thinking. That is the wrong motive.

If the highest ambition you have for your children is to go to college and get a good education so they can get a good job and pay bills, get rid of that vision and get a bigger one for them. Dream of them going to college and getting an education in order to own companies and create jobs for other people, as well as always have enough to give God.

The Bible says train up a child in the right way, and when that child is an adult, he will not depart from those ways. (Prov. 22:6.) The very next verse says that the one who borrows is servant to the one who lends. If you buy your child his first car on credit, you are training him to live by the debt-system.

Most parents say, "If you work to pay the monthly payment, you can have the car," and think they are training that child right.

Why not train your child to pay cash? Why train your children up in debt? Tell him that, if he works and saves his money, you will chip in an equal amount (or whatever you can) and pay cash for a car. He will get a better deal and begin to think about finances in a sound, godly way.

Also, do you figure tithe on the "net" or the "gross"? The net is the amount you take home, after Uncle Sam, the state, and local governments get theirs.

The *gross* is the total amount you actually make, although you never see close to twenty-five percent of it.

God says, "My part is the firstfruits of the total, the full salary before deductions."

The more I give God, the more He blesses me, and the more He blesses me, the more I can give Him percentage-wise. I am believing to get to the place where we can give ninety percent and live abundantly and prosperously on ten.

A Summary of Principles of Giving

The first principle is this: All the tithe does is get you *ready* to receive. You cannot give someone a gift of something that does not belong to you. Tithe is not yours to give; it already belongs to God. So does everything else you own, but He only claims ten percent back as a constant, given principle.

Also, remember to figure God's percentage on the total. He is to get the firstfruits. If you pay taxes and social security, *then* give God His, He is not getting the "firstfruits" but the "second-fruits."

Offerings are up to you, but they should be given out of a willing, generous heart. The amount and place to sow them should be at the Holy Spirit's direction.

The second aspect is that *sowing and reaping* is God's system of enabling you to make a profit. The more you invest, the more "interest" you receive. Concerning sowing and reaping, there are several points to remember:

1. You must sow into good soil which the Master chooses.

2. You must sow "good" seed of whatever you want back.

3. You must "water" the seed with the Word.

4. You must keep the "weeds" (doubt, unbelief, and so forth) out of your crop.

5. You must expect a harvest.

Sowing into good soil means giving to the ministry, church, missions, or individuals that are alive and doing something real for God. Also, it means knowing that He has put it in your heart to sow there. Giving into some old, dry, wrinkled-up work means you are sowing on stony ground, and your seed will not live, much less return a harvest.

No farmer will just walk out onto rocks and dry, desert ground and begin to scatter seeds around. The birds will eat them, or the wind will blow them away. They are wasted. Good ground has been worked, plowed and fertilized, and watered with prayers and the anointing of the Holy Spirit.

If I happen to be in a church where no light is being produced, I keep my money in my wallet. Only in good ground are you guaranteed a thirty-, sixty-, or hundred-fold return. The best return you get in the world's system is twenty-five percent, and usually it is less.

Giving to a man of God, who really is called, anointed, and moving for God, is giving into good soil. In the Old Testament, the priests were to get the offerings.

I have had people walk up to me and say, "God told me to give this to you, and He would bless me for it."

All I did was receive it "as unto the Lord," and spend it on whatever need I had. And the Lord did bless them. Some of those people are still walking in blessings from what they gave. Invest in God's work or God's man (or woman), and your "bread" will come back to you on the waters of time.

You are no different than the widow at Zarephath, whom God called to give her last piece of bread to Elijah. (1 Kings 17:8-24.) God is no respector of persons. He honors obedience and willingness to obey His principles. His Word is true.

Good seed means money *offered* from the right motive. Money is not evil in itself. If you earn money in any illegal way, then get saved and dedicate yourself and your possessions to God, your money is "saved" as well. However, you cannot offer money to God out of wrong motives, including ill-gained funds to salve your conscience, and have it be "good seed" that will bring in a harvest.

Proverbs 3:9 says to **honor the Lord with thy substance, and with the firstfruits of all thine increase.** Another translation would be to "honor the Lord with your capital and with everything earned by righteous labor." Gambling is not "righteous labor." Winnings from Las Vegas are not "righteous winnings." Also, do not rob or cheat someone, then bring God the tithe to make your conscience feel better.

Good seed also means that anything you give away must be in as good a condition as possible. If you give away junk, you will get junk back. Like produces like: That is another law of God. If you want a harvest of money, sow money. If you need clothes, give out of your need, and you will get clothes returned.

If you give someone a car, make sure it is running. Invest in it first. I like what Evangelist Kenneth Copeland does. If he gives away an airplane, he has a standing policy with the recipient. If something goes wrong with it, they can bring it back, and he has it fixed.

Each time he has given away a car or plane, God has given him a better one. When you give away good stuff, God will give you good stuff in return. If you give away clothes — even ones you have worn can be *good* clothes — make sure they are mended, buttons and zippers all on, and even cleaned and ironed.

Watering the seed means praising the Lord for the return, thanking Him in advance for the harvest, as a Christian farmer does from seed-planting time to harvest. The "weeds" to keep out are: doubt, unbelief, strife and contention with your spouse or family, impatience (pulling up your seed to see if it's growing), resentment of others who seem to be getting faster or better returns than you, unforgiveness, and other negative thoughts and attitudes. Any of those will limit, or even abort, your harvest.

Expect to receive your harvest. As soon as you decide to give a certain amount over the tithe, more than likely, things break down, or unexpected expenses come up to pull you off your decision. But give anyway and expect your harvest.

In the next chapter, I want to show you how your attitude toward the leaders set in the Body of Christ affect your harvest. Wrongful attitudes can allow weeds to grow or crows to come and steal the harvest.

7
The Right Attitude Toward Leadership

Many Christians do not have the right attitude toward leadership. Because those in the five-fold offices are the voice of Jesus to His Church (along with the voice of the Holy Spirit), disrepect or a contemptuous attitude toward them causes God's hand to be closed over your life. Anytime God is prevented from blessing you or answering your prayers by attacks of the enemy (Dan. 10:13) or by wrong attitudes (Matt. 11:25,26), usually your finances are hit first.

This is because, although God owns all the wealth, the world systems are set up and under the authority of "Mammon." So that is the easiest place for the devil to attack individuals, groups, or countries. The second easiest place is in relationships between people or countries.

It is not required of you to "obey" leadership if they are asking you to do something against your conscience, teaching doctrines that are against Scripture, or coming out with the wrong attitude. What is required is *respect for the office.* If the man in the office is wrong, pray for him. Seek God about attending a different church. Especially do not try to plant financial seed in a place that has a "dead" or "religious" leader.

That person is not truly representing God, neither is someone in ministry for the money. He is a "hireling."

However, look at the life of David, Israel's first king of the line of Judah. Even when King Saul was trying to kill him, and David had been anointed already as the true king, David always was careful to give Saul the respect due one of "the Lord's anointed." As long as Saul was alive, he was in the office and still God's anointed. (1 Sam. 24:1-10.)

Then David's wife, Michal, not only had contempt for him when he danced in the streets, but she rebuked and corrected him in that attitude. (2 Sam. 6:20-23.) Her *attitude toward leadership* is what caused her to remain childless the rest of her life and to be put away as the king's wife.

She would not have been out of line, if she had gently said, "Honey, do you think perhaps the king ought not to be dancing in the streets with common folk? Do you think that may cause them to disrespect the office?"

Or, better still, she could have gone to the Lord about it and trusted Him to deal with David on such matters, if David was wrong.

On the other hand, if she had not been his wife, an advisor (a member of his "cabinet"), or a prophet sent by God, she would have had no right to say anything to him at all. She would only have been right if she prayed.

America is a nation of rebels. We were founded in a revolt, a revolution against authority. That does not mean we should not have seceded from England, but it does mean that independence has been bred into us for more than two hundred years. We are taught it in school, and since the Sixties, that has escalated into a spirit of rebellion against authority.

Today, the government bows down to various groups in rebellion and tries to please them. So the rebellion-against-establishment has turned against the Church. The Charismatic movement brought in many of the generation of rebellion, and their attitudes have carried over into their Christian lives.

Most of the time, when people see pastors, evangelists, prophets, and teachers, they see the prestige of the office — but they do not see the responsibility involved. If you can truly understand the purpose and plan of God when he calls men and women to "stand in the gap" for His people and to be His voice in the earth, you will not easily fall into a disrespectful or contemptuous attitude, no matter how badly you feel those people are handling things.

Instead of criticizing and condemning, you will stay on your face praying for them. They need it.

You may be thinking, "But I do not come against leadership."

Do you ever begrudge offerings for the pastor? Does your church keep the pastor and his family on "minimum wages"? Do you allow the thought that ministers are only in the ministry "to get money"? If so, then you have a wrong attitude toward those sent by God.

The Bible says if you receive a prophet as a prophet, you get a prophet's reward. (Matt. 10:41.) The same is true of the other offices. No one is perfect, and it is so easy to judge those up in front. Better think whether you could do any better if it were you. Also, if you *do* think you can do better, watch out — that is the beginning of an "Absalom spirit."

Absalom was reared by David and was his own son, yet he led a revolt against him, because he pridefully thought he could do better. The problem was, God had not anointed him for the king's office.

God's Pattern for Ministry

This may not sound as if it is about wealth, but it is. Exodus 23:15 says no one should come before God empty-handed, and Numbers 18:1,5 is the pattern for those standing in God's offices:

> **And the Lord said unto Aaron, thou and thy sons and thy father's house with thee shall bear the iniquity of the sanctuary:** (that is, the guilt for the offense which the people unknowingly commit when brought into contact with the manifestations of God's presence) **and thou and thy sons with thee shall bear the iniquity of your priesthood.**
>
> **And ye shall keep the charge of the sanctuary, and the charge of the altar: that there be no wrath any more upon the children of Israel.**

That chapter contains some of the most awesome statements you will ever read in the entire Bible. God made a decision to pick out one man and his family and make them responsible for an entire nation's sins.

God was saying to Aaron, "Whenever someone sins against me, you are responsible to intercede for them and make sure the proper sacrifices are made on their behalf. You are responsible for making sure that when they come to me in an attitude of forgiveness they come in the right way. And you are to present their sacrifices to me in the way I have ordained, so that I can forgive them."

Now, I understand all of that was a "picture" or a type of the real Mediator to come, Jesus Christ, and I understand that each of us is responsible to God personally. No longer can any man stand between you and a personal responsibility to go through Jesus for forgiveness of sins.

However, there is another side of this that Christians overlook. They assume that a personal relationship with God makes them "Lone Rangers" with each man having as much spiritual authority as another and each person having the same right to make decisions for God as another. And that totally overlooks the other aspect of God's plan for His people — the Church.

You become a member of God's family through a personal relationship with Jesus, through accepting His sacrifice for the penalty of spiritual death that hung over you through Adam and Eve. You are responsible for going straight to the Father through Jesus if you have sinned as a child of His.

However, when you accepted Jesus, you became a member of His Body and *within the Body on earth* God has set certain offices as authority to pass on His directions for the corporate family. *That has nothing to do with individual sins.* The authority of the five-fold offices has to do with overall direction, overall revelation, and responsibility for the "souls" (personal development in spiritual maturity) of those assigned to them.

There is a seriousness associated with being in leadership. People's lives are at stake depending on what a pastor tells them, or how he counsels them from God. I have found that the closer I get to God, the less He will put up with from me. I am finding out God's ways.

Moses knew God's ways, and the Israelites saw God's acts. If they really had spent time learning His ways, they would have seen more acts in love than judgment. To some of the Israelites, Moses' office looked glamorous — just as televangelists do today to some people. But very few of them, and very few Christians, see the awesome responsibility placed on a leader who stands in an office for God.

God is a God of grace, but after a certain period of probation, grace turns to judgment. Then you had better just get out of the way. Most modern Christians ought to be thankful that judgment does not immediately fall for coming against His offices as it did on Miriam when she criticized Moses for marrying an Ethiopian wife! She was struck almost instantly with leprosy, and she was Moses' sister. (Num. 12:1-16.) Relative or not, she had no *right* to set herself up in judgment over a leader. There are other examples in the story of the Israelites of immediate judgment for rebelling, even murmuring, against a leader. (Num. 16:1-35,46-50; 21:5-9)

God takes it very seriously when you do not respect those offices He has placed in the Church. He has a divine order that He expects us to respect.

You may say, ''But we are not under Aaron and the priesthood. We are not under the Old Covenant.'' Well, let me show you God's *specific* literal instructions from the New Testament.

> **Obey them that have the rule** (authority) **over you, and submit yourselves: for they watch for your souls, as they that must give account, that they may do it with joy, and not with grief: for that is unprofitable for you.**
>
> **Hebrews 13:17**

I wonder how many pastors know they are to give an account for the souls (minds, wills, emotions) of their members? I wonder how many members know this? I have to stand before God one day, and I did not ask God for this job. I was drafted! My soul would prefer to be a chief executive officer somewhere! But God said He wanted me to preach.

Church Membership Is Not an Option

When I began to see this, the Holy Spirit said to me, "Son, people have not understood the ramifications of membership in a church. They still think that is an option — something they can do whenever they feel like it. Anyone who does that is playing Russian roulette with his life. One of the greatest punishments that can happen to a born-again believer is to be put out of a church."

He took me to 1 Corinthians 5:1-5 where a man was committing incest with his stepmother. The Apostle Paul, the top spiritual authority *on earth* to the Corinthian church, wrote that he had already judged the man. He directed the local members to "turn that man's flesh over to the devil for destruction that his soul might be saved."

What they did was kick the "dude" out of the church and treat him as a heathen, who had no part in the family of God. They would have nothing to do with him.

The Lord showed me that when you are not connected in the natural to another part of the Body you do not have a "covering" — someone who can look out for you, stand in the gap for you and intercede for you. At that point, you are open territory for the devil.

So having yourself connected to a local church is not an option, it is a necessity. You cannot walk in the fullness of your blessings when you are floating here and there, trying to find the perfect church. *There are none.* The pastor's job is to look after his people, intercede on their behalf, and communicate to them the Word and the principles of God. His responsibility is to bring them to the point where they *can* go straight to God through the Holy Spirit, repent, and be forgiven.

Paul said of those not saved, "How can they be saved if they do not hear the Word, and how can they hear the Word, if someone is not sent?" (Rom. 10:15.) The same thing is true of spiritual growth.

Because God does not immediately judge us today for coming against God's anointed or attempting to usurp their authority does not mean God is not taking disrespect as seriously. If you study the rest of the Levite pattern, you will see there are certain places only the pastor can "touch."

Again, let me say that I understand we are under Jesus, who is a Priest of the Order of Melchizedek (Heb. 6:20); however, God's principles never change. The natural order has changed, in that we have Jesus in Heaven as our High Priest and final authority and not a man on earth. But in the New Testament, we see in 1 Corinthians that *God* Himself set spiritual representatives in the Body as authorities.

In the Old Testament, priests were called gifts (Num. 18:6) to the Body of the time (Israel), and in the New Testament, the five-fold offices and other offices are called "gifts." (1 Cor. 12:1-9.)

They no longer have the responsibility of sacrificing animals for you — you go straight to the One

Who is the Sacrifice, once and for all. Nevertheless, the five-fold offices still have a tremendous responsibility, and as God's "sent one," (which is what *anointed* means), they are due respect as God's ambassadors.

When you try to take the lead in your church and run things, usurping the authority of your pastor and elders, or when you talk about them behind their backs, or when you stir up strife and contention within the church against them, you are coming against the Holy Spirit. And, indeed, we are fortunate today that many of us do not drop dead!

Learn to submit to authority, then perhaps, you will be ready for God to use you in a leadership position. Paul wrote Timothy not to use new converts in positions of authority because it might go to their heads. (1 Tim. 3:6.) First they needed to be trained by submitting to a man of God. Again, we look to the Old Testament for the pattern, and that is Elijah and Elisha. The younger man served faithfully and apparently uncomplainingly for at least ten years before receiving the mantle of the older prophet.

When the office of pastor is not respected, the person in the office cannot completely fulfill his duties. He can only "oversee" the souls of those who will allow it. (Again, let me make it clear that I am not talking about someone misusing his office to put Christians in bondage.) There are a lot of pastors out there, I am afraid, who were not called. They just wanted a church, and they treat the pastorate as a career.

And there are too many churchgoers who feel they are "just as good" as the pastor and have a right to judge him, correct him, and kick him out if he does not please them. His responsibility is to please God, not the members. The individual Christian has a responsibility to judge the teaching and preaching that comes forth, but they are to judge it against the Bible *not against their own thoughts, traditions, or doctrines.*

Do as the Bereans did and search the scriptures diligently to see the truth of what you are being taught. (Acts 17:11.) However, you will never find in the Old or New Testaments that it is okay for you to judge *God's man or woman,* only their works and their words (by the Word and the Holy Spirit).

Part of the respect for the office is attitude, part is behavior — doing whatever you can to help in the church, and part is making sure the pastor is taken care of the way God wants him to be. That means finances. Many pastors have gone out and gotten jobs to take care of their families. They have had to, because their members would not release the money to pay them. Rather than hear the criticism, the pastors work.

One of the saddest passages in Scripture is when the Levites had to go back to work on a secular job after the return of the Jews from exile. Nehemiah came to Jerusalem, and said, "Enough is enough. Get this straightened out. Bring your tithes and offerings into the temple. (Neh. 13:9-13.) You cannot have the nation restored until you get the priesthood working right."

As the Head Goes, So Goes the Body

You cannot walk in wealth unless you have the right attitude towards leadership in the church, and that means seeing that the needs of leadership are met. "As the head goes, so goes the body" is an old saying, but it is true.

Blessings come to those who make sure God's people are taken care of. He will bless the work of your hands when you bless the men and women of God, who are standing in the gap for you and watching over your soul. A pastor is to pray for the people, and God meets their spiritual needs through him. Then God wants to meet the pastor's natural needs through the people.

The pattern in the Old Testament shows that those who served in the temple got their food from the temple, and those who served at the altar shared in the offerings brought. In the New Testament, Jesus said the laborer is worthy of his hire. (Luke 10:7.)

As your leader goes, so go you. If he has been held back from blessings, so will his members be — because *you are connected.* The Head of the total Body is Jesus. If He were not blessed, then we could not be. If the head of the local church is not blessed, then neither can the members of the body be blessed. If your leader is not prospering, then you cannot.

God gave Aaron charge of the ''heave offering'' forever. (Num. 18:10,11.) God said whatever offerings the people brought to Him, He gave back to the priests. He called them to full-time service; therefore, He was to provide for them. His way of providing was through the people, so that the people could sow seed to receive a harvest for themselves.

The divine plan is a cycle: the people gave to God, and through Him, to the priests who served them. Then, because of willing obedience, God was able to rebuke the devourer for their sakes, meet their needs, and multiply their offerings back to them. That is God's overall principle for His people in any age. In the Old Testament, it was carried out in one way — offerings of wheat and meat, and so forth. Today, God operates through the collection plate.

In rural areas of America until modern times, people still brought food, meat, produce, and so forth to the pastors. Usually, they brought the best they had, because money was scarce. This was done on a voluntary basis, because after the New Covenant was ratified, the "law" is written on our hearts. We know from the Holy Spirit (if we really listen) that we are to take care of those who meet our spiritual needs.

Many Christians today, however, do not receive all they should from their pastors because they *will* not minister to their needs. Unfortunately, most Christians also do not want to even ask the pastor's advice, even on marriage. They will ask the pastor to marry them, but at the same time, want him to keep his mouth shut about whether he feels this is the right thing to do.

Most pastors would like any parishioners planning marriage to come in for counseling before the wedding.

The attitude usually is, "Well, I'll go in and get this out of the way. It's just part of getting married, like the wedding ceremony. But no matter what he says, I'm going to marry her anyway."

God said to "consult your leader." But most people do not want to hear advice or counsel, unless it agrees with what they already want to do. Deuteronomy 17:8,9 is still God's principles for His people:

> **If there arise a matter too hard for thee in judgment, between blood and blood** (one kind of bloodshed and another), **between plea and plea** (one legality and another), **and between stroke and stroke** (one kind of assault and another), **being matters of controversy within thy gates: then shalt thou arise, and get thee up into the place** (in our day, the church) **which the Lord thy God shall choose;**

And thou shalt come unto the priests the Levites, and unto the judge that shall be in those days, and inquire; and they shall shew thee the sentence of judgment (make clear to you the decision).

That is where a lot of people miss it. They do not consult the pastor until after the fact. Most people do not consult their pastors, because they know already what they want to do is wrong, inadvisable, or against God's purposes for them — but they want to do whatever it is anyway. They do not want to hear anything negative.

So they do not come to their pastors until they have made messes out of their lives. Then they want help. Then they want to know why God let them do it. He let them, because they did not go to the offices He has set in the Body to help them. They did not really want help, they wanted to do what they pleased.

Not just marriages, but business deals are things you need to get a confirmation on from your spiritual leader. In addition to seeking God in your best interests, someone on the outside looking in can see things clearer than you, because you are right in the middle of the situation.

Deuteronomy 17:10-12 continues:

And thou shalt do according to the sentence (decision), **which they of that place which the Lord shall choose shall shew thee; and thou shalt observe to do according to all that they inform thee:**

According to the sentence (decision) **of the law which they shall teach thee, and according to the judgment which they shall tell thee, thou shalt do: thou shalt decline from the sentence** (not turn aside from the verdict they give you) **which they shall shew thee, to the right hand, nor to the left.**

And the man that will *do presumptuously*, and will not hearken unto the priest that standeth to minister there before the Lord thy God, or unto the judge, even that man shall die. . . .

Give as Unto the Lord

The man or woman today who does not belong to a church or does not consult the pastor on serious matters is *doing presumptuously*, according to the Word. We have a "better covenant," but that does not mean we have more spiritual leniency. It simply means we have no one set over us in the natural to *force* us to keep God's law. The fact that we have more freedom of choice puts *more* responsibility on us to make the right choices. And, to do that, the Bible says to seek counsel. Seek a confirmation, and the first person to start with is the spiritual leader who has been set over your soul.

When you give offerings, you need to understand that *you* are not giving to the pastor. You are giving to God, and *He* is giving to the pastor. God told the Israelites that He could quite easily have taken their firstborn sons when He took Egypt's, but that because He spared their children, they owed Him their children. Instead of the children being set aside for service to God, the Lord took the tribe of Levites.

He said, "Rather than taking everyone's firstborn for My service, I will set Levi apart to me, and they will be in your stead." Every time a firstborn son is birthed, I will see the Levites, and they will be to me a wave (peace) offering. Every time I see the Levites, I understand that the entire nation of Israel is at peace with me, because the Levites will be out in front of the sanctuary interceding on your behalf. Aaron and his sons will be on the inside interceding on your behalf."

Whatever offerings the people brought to God, He gave to the Levites because He was the one who had called them. Therefore He was providing for them, *but through the people,* as I pointed out earlier in this chapter. All of the offerings to God were supposed to be the best and the firstfruits.

Instead of giving their firstborn child or the "firstlings" of unclean beasts, the people could substitute silver. Today, it is no different. God called His ministers, so He provides for them through the people. If the people disobeyed in Old Testament times and brought offerings that were not up to par — then the priests suffered.

If this kept on long enough, God called the nation to account.

Today, many ministers suffer because the whole Body is not giving God His portion, much less the offerings that go to His ministers. There will come an accounting. In fact, I believe that is a big part of the reason for America's inflation and depression cycle during this century. The Body cannot be blessed if those set in offices to represent God are not blessed.

Nehemiah reminded the returned exiles of the offerings due God, and he commanded them to give the portion due the priests and Levites that they might be free to give themselves to study of the Word. As soon as the command went abroad, the people responded in abundance. (Neh. 13:12.)

There are more scriptures in the New Testament that clearly show God has never changed in the way He provides for His servants.

> **Let him who receives instruction in the Word [of God] share all good things with his teacher [contributing to his support].**
>
> **Galatians 6:6 AMP**

Let the elders who perform the duties of their office well be considered doubly worthy of honor [and of adequate financial support], especially those who labor faithfully in preaching and teaching.
1 Timothy 5:17 AMP

Who serves as a soldier at his own expense? When you went into the service, did you have to take money and supply your own clothes? Did you have to buy your own weapons? No — the government who called you provided your arms, clothes, and equipment. The government (and really the funds for all this come from the people) houses and feeds those who fight for the country.

The key to overcoming this area of wrong attitude to authority is to study the Word of God and *change the way you think.* You are and have what you think. If you have any of these thoughts about pastors, about churches, and about giving — research the Bible as I did, and *change* your thoughts to God's thoughts.

8

Learn How To Be a Good Steward

Organization is one of the key principles to receiving God's blessings in your life. If you are a sloppy person, you will have a hard time receiving. I have found that God is even interested in whether or not you have your clothes sorted and lined up neatly in dresser drawers!

God is interested in whether you can get in and out of your closet without stuff falling down on you. He is interested in knowing whether you can get in and out of your garage. Many people have their garages so full of junk piled in them that they cannot even get their cars inside.

God operates in orderliness, and He wants us to do so.

In Genesis 1:1, the Bible says God *created* the heavens and the earth. Then in verse 2, something odd occurs. The earth is said to be without form and void; in other words, in chaos. How could God have created chaos? He is a God of order.

Most Bible scholars believe, from other passages, that God created the earth perfect. Then the conflict with Satan and his angels occurred, and in the process, the earth was involved in some cataclysm that left it "without form and void," which in the Hebrew, means "an empty, formless waste."

In the last part of verse 2, Moses told us that the Spirit of God began to move on the face of the waters. What happened then was that God began to bring order out of chaos. From verse 2 to verse 26, you do not find the Hebrew word for *create*, which means to make something new.

It is very uncharacteristic of God to start out with order in verse one and end up with chaos in verse 2. *Chaos* also means "confusion," and that is not of God. If the earth was created perfect in the beginning, which is how God does everything that He does, then why would it have been "a confused, empty waste" in verse 2?

Void also means "indistinguishable." One thing was not able to be distinguished from another. You could not make heads or tails out of it. Another definition is "disorder." God creates order, not disorder. Therefore, if the earth was in confusion, it was not God's doing.

Also, God not only does not change, He does not lose. Whatever happened to the earth between the original creation and the time when God saw the earth formless and void did not stop God's plan. He is never defeated. At the right time, He began to bring order out of chaos.

What God did on the first six days of creation was call forth things from what already existed. At the end of the sixth day, however, there is that word for *create* again, used in connection with man.

How can God bless you with more money if what you have is in chaos?

How can God give you more finances to handle if you have not handled rightly what you already have?

Can you give an account of every penny you receive?

The Bible says God is not the author of confusion (1 Cor. 14:33), which means the devil is. God will not bless confusion. If He is not the author of something, He does not have to bless it. Many Christians' lives, much less their homes, are in a state of complete chaos.

If you do not have a plan for the wealth, God is not going to give it to you. When you begin to get organized, God will release more blessings in your life. It is what you are doing with what you already have that makes the big difference.

If you are not an organized and faithful steward over what God has given you, then He will not put any more in your hands. The Bible says that, instead, He will take what you have and give it to someone who *is* faithful. (Matt. 25:26-30.)

First Corinthians 4:2 says:

> **Moreover it is required in stewards, that a man be found faithful.**

Essential means "necessary," and when God says something is *required*, that thing is not optional. That means, in order to receive according to the promise, you must do things exactly as He said.

Required means you cannot do what you want to, nor the way you want to do it.

Taking Dominion Is Stewardship

Stewards are those who care for someone else's property. We already have seen that everything belongs to God. We do not own anything, we simply have the use of our possessions. What God intended was for mankind to be *stewards* over His earth and His material resources. That is what having "dominion" means.

You can also see this truth from several parables Jesus told, likening God to the Master or Owner, and His people to servants or stewards. His parables plainly describe the difference between wicked and faithful stewards.

We are to be stewards of God's property. Everything on earth is subject to us, because the Boss already gave the order. In Genesis 1:26,28, God said, "Man, I am giving you dominion over the earth and over everything that walks, crawls, or creeps."

We are to bring the earth under our authority. *Dominion* includes money. Paul's statement to the Corinthians that stewards must be found *faithful* means they must be "trustworthy."

Let me ask you a few questions that will show you whether or not you operate in discipline and organization:

*Do you have a budget, planned on a weekly or monthly basis?

*Do you make a grocery list of what you need that will stay within your weekly budget? Or do you go into the store and buy on impulse, perhaps spending a lot more than you should?

*Do you have scheduled maintenance for your car?

God watches how you take care of your car, because that is not yours either. If you drive ninety thousand miles without changing the oil, then when the car stops on you, you try to lay hands on it in faith for it to run — God is not going to answer you.

If you cannot do things yourself, there are people out there qualified to service cars, clean houses and organize closets, and so forth. If you cannot do something, believe for enough money or budget the money to hire someone else to do it. *But take care of what God has given you if you want more!*

And sometimes, you are asking God for more money when you already have what you need for the time being. You just do not have it in order and arranged properly. God is not going to bring tremendous wealth to your house if what you already have is not organized.

This is even more important than simply getting wealth. God equates your ability to rule with your ability to handle finances. Do you want to rule and reign with Him? Then you must learn to "rule" over the little that you have, in order to gain much.

God dealt with me personally over this principle. I know for sure He is concerned about how organized you keep your dresser drawers. Prior to a little over a year ago, my dresser drawers were chaotic. Then I heard pastor, teacher, and author Myles Munroe from the Bahamas teach on purpose and organization.

What the Holy Spirit revealed through him began to burn in my spirit. I came home, and my wife did not know what had happened to me. I started throwing away all the old socks and underwear that had holes in them. If you men are like me, you might be coming to church with holes in your socks, and it would be embarrassing if a footwashing had been scheduled!

I began to organize my things and fold them up neatly. It took me about a week to complete that process. Then I went out and started on the garage.

Among other things, I bought something on which to roll up my one hundred-foot electrical cord, instead of throwing it down. It is amazing how much stuff you can throw away. Some of you readers are where I was then.

After seeing my example, my wife also got more organized. Almost immediately we saw our bills begin to be met. We went quickly from running two or three months behind to being current. You would not think organization would have that much effect on paying your bills — but it did. That is how I know God honors your coming into organization and discipline.

He even considers us stewards over socks and shoes. If we are not faithful to show appreciation by taking care of little things, why should he give us more? If you want a really nice car, keep up the one you have. Even if it clanks when you drive it, keep it clean.

When Jesus fed the thousands with loaves and fishes, He had them sit down in orderly rows, groups of fifties and one hundreds. Why did He do that? If He had not made them sit in orderly groups and wait for food to be handed out, some people might have gotten hurt or killed! There would have been a stampede to get the food. People are always afraid someone else is going to get ahead of them or get what belongs to them.

Churches Need Organization

Moses had to learn to organize. He was trying to handle all of the complaints and problems of more than a million people! God had to send his father-in-law, Jethro, to advise him to organize a chain of command to handle civil affairs. (Ex. 18:13-24.)

> And Moses chose able men out of all Israel, and made them heads over the people, rulers of thousands, rulers of hundreds, rulers of fifties, and rulers of tens.
>
> And they judged the people at all seasons: the hard causes they brought unto Moses, but every small matter they judged themselves.
>
> Exodus 18:25,26

Every pastor needs to learn from Moses that, as his church or ministry grows larger, he needs an organizational structure. The Lord said to me, "Order, structure, and foundation." When He speaks like that, you do something! So we began to organize the church.

We named pastors for various areas of service, people to whom we could delegate all down the line. We established policies for each part of the ministry and church. We laid down requirements for those who would become members or workers in each area.

In some divisions, you should have been a member of the church long enough to establish your faithfulness. In others, you need to have a certain amount of Bible training. You cannot be a novice. Paul wrote Timothy not to use new converts for positions of authority because it might go to their heads. (1 Tim. 3:6.) They would not be able to handle the responsibility rightly.

The root of the word *disciple* is *discipline*. A lot of Christians are running around with no discipline in their lives. Therefore, they cannot be true disciples of Jesus. They are not following Him if they are into confusion, chaos, and disorder.

There are a lot of "renegade" Christians today who do not want to submit to authority. However, in the times just ahead, you will learn to come under the

Holy Spirit's direction and that of those He sets over you in the fivefold offices, or you will be outside watching the rest of the Church move on.

God does not accept renegade Christians. If you will not submit to earthly authority, you will not submit to heavenly authority. Please understand, I am not writing about authority that amounts to "bondage," but I am talking about recognizing offices as people sent by God to you. I am talking about spiritual authority operating by mandate of the Holy Spirit.

Also, part of being under spiritual authority is to be committed to a particular church or ministry. Just make sure the Holy Spirit is assigning you there, and that the church is going somewhere and is not dead. If every Sunday is like a funeral, you need to leave that church. However, if you are placed there by the Lord, you can stay in peace, even if you do not like or agree with everything that is said or done.

Nowhere in the Bible are we told, "Do not forsake fellowshipping together unless you don't like the pastor, or you don't like the music, or you don't like the other people who go there."

A "renegade" Christian is one who is under no one's authority but skips and hops from place to place. God has a hard time blessing those people, because they are not connected to a vision. "Renegade" Christians are "Lone Rangers," and God does not call anyone to be that. Everyone has his place in the Body.

You will never find the "perfect" church, one that is exactly the way you would like it to be. That is because you are not the only one attending. If it could be the way you chose, everyone else in that church would have to be "clones" of you. Then it certainly would not be perfect, would it?

Find one that teaches the Word, exalts the name of Jesus, and lives as sanctified as they know how. They are permitting God to be God. Get in that place, and put down some roots. Get connected to the vision there. Then God will be able to bear some fruit from your branches.

If the pastor or leaders are not what they are supposed to be in your estimation — pray for them! Do not judge, criticize, or talk about them.

If all of the saints there do not speak to you and act friendly, pray for them. You need to be connected to some vision of God.

God also wants your food and your time to be put in order, as well as your finances and property.

Diet and Schedules Need To Be in Order

If you live a fasted lifestyle, you will always have your life in order. I tell my body when it can eat and when it cannot. I eat only when I need to in order to keep the body in good health and energy, and I eat only as much as I know I need. I live a fasted lifestyle.

When you do that, your life is always under control. Also, it helps you to hear God any time. When the body is indulged and heavy with food, you do not hear the Lord as well.

With a fasted lifestyle, you can eat the things you want — just not eat as much of them. The Apostle Paul's instruction about food was "to eat what is set before you." (1 Cor. 10:27.) He did not tell us to eat enough greens, or to make sure we ate samples of the four food groups each day.

When he said, "Eat what is before you," that meant, "Bless whatever food is provided for you, and it will nourish your body."

Food is sanctified by the Word and prayer. Some people pray over the main meals, but forget about the snacks. I guarantee you that if you prayed over every snack, you might not eat as many snacks!

I have come to the place where food does not matter. We need to stop putting guilt trips on our children because they do not eat everything on their plates. Why tell them there are starving kids in India, so "you better eat *your* spinach"?

There are starving children in India, but your children becoming gluttons will not help them! Naturally, you need to train children not to take more than they can eat, if possible. But you can take even a good principle to the extreme and turn it into a bad one. You can instill in children a compulsion to eat, even though your *motives* are the best in the world. It is your *methods* that are misguided.

When you take care of the body, the enemy cannot put anything on you. The devil has tried to attack my heart from so many different angles.

But when he attacks, I say, "You're out of your mind. I don't receive it. I don't accept it. You can't put it on me," and I begin to quote the Word to him.

The only time he can attack you is when you abuse the body through lack of rest, allowing stress to run, or eating wrongly. The Church needs to get rid of the idea that God kills people. Jesus already has provided health for you. Your part is to appropriate that and take authority over your body.

Another area God looks at to see if you are organized in is the area of *time*. Ephesians 5:16 says we should be **redeeming the time, because the days are evil.** If the days were evil in Paul's lifetime, how much more so in ours.

Your time is as precious as your money. When you are born, you are allotted so many minutes, hours, and days. Each time you "spend" one, that is one that you will never be able to replace. "Redeeming the time" means making the most of it. Do not waste your time. Let your moments of existence be useful.

If I am driving, rather than just floating along, I try to redeem that time by playing Bible tapes or ministry tapes. I use that time to put more Word in my spirit and mind. If I am in the gym exercising, being a good steward over my body, I also will have on earphones "redeeming the time" by listening to some more Word.

All of your "spare" time (over the job, housework, and so forth) should not be spent gossipping on the phone, window shopping in the mall, or watching some sport or entertainment show on television. God has no problem with you doing that occasionally. However, if that is what consumes your time, your time is out of order.

I also found that, as I began to organize my life and bring it in line with God, the anointing also increased. I found that God began to give me more responsibility as a pastor. He put more in my hands to do.

The parable of the talents in Matthew 25, or the parable of the ten servants in Luke 19, involved money. "Talents" were not skills or abilities, but coins. And when the nobleman returned from receiving the kingdom for which he went into a far country, he said to the man who invested one talent and made ten in return:

"Well done! You are a good and faithful servant. Because you have been trustworthy over a little, now

I am going to give you authority over ten cities.'' (Luke 19:15-17.)

What does being a good investor of money have to do with authority over cities? Money is only a servant, and if you are not able to have authority over money, then you will not be able to exercise authority over a city.

Money is a servant. It is supposed to work for you. This story, along with other passages, shows that God equates your being able to handle finances with you being able to rule and reign. If your finances are out of control, that means they are running you. You are not ruling over them. You are the servant of money, in bondage to ''Mammon,'' instead of money being your servant.

The best soil in which to invest, of course, is the spreading of the Gospel.

The bottom line is this: If you are not disciplined and in control of your soul and body, it is hard for God to release wealth into your hands. If you have not been a good steward over your body, your income, and the possessions you now have, God will not trust you with more.

9

Vows and Memorial Offerings

One of the most awesome things you will read in the Bible is that God said He magnified His Word over His name. He counts His Word of more value than even His name. (Ps. 138:2.) I have found the reason for that is: If your word is not worth anything, neither is your name. All God has ever asked of us is a verbal contract.

His covenant is established with His people through His Word and theirs. He invites you to come to Him through the Holy Spirit, and you accept by "confessing" with your mouth (tongue) that Jesus died for you and was resurrected to sit at the right hand of the Father. (Rom. 9:9,10.)

When you give verbal agreement to something, in essence, you are "vowing a vow." I want to explain the place of vows and memorial offerings in a Christian's life.

You will find two kinds of vows in the Word of God: conditional and unconditional.

A *conditional* vow is when you make a verbal contract with God. If He will do something, you will do something. Some people call it "making a bargain" with God. However, you cannot bargain with God!

You *can* make an individual, specific covenant with Him, as long as what you are asking is within His will. He said that He was a "covenant" God (Deut. 7:9), One who keeps covenant and mercy with those who love and obey Him. That means He does everything by His word, by promises and decrees.

An *unconditional* vow says, "Lord, I'm going to do this because I love You."

A conditional vow is the kind Hannah made with God, if He would give her a son. In the Middle East at that time, a woman with no children, particularly no sons, was of little value. If her husband did not care about her, she was in big trouble.

Hannah's husband loved her. In fact, he said, "Am I not more to you than ten sons?" (1 Sam. 1:8.) But his other wife had several children and made fun of Hannah. So every year, when they went up for the annual sacrifices (which, before the temple was built, were held at Shiloh), she wept and travailed to God for a son. (1 Sam. 1:3.)

Finally, one year she could not take it anymore, so she "vowed a vow" to God that if He would give her a son, she would give that son back to Him to serve the Lord "all his days." (1 Sam. 1:11.) She prayed and cried so hard that Eli, the high priest of the time, thought she was drunk. He rebuked her, telling her to "put away her wine."

The words from her mouth, however, were not indignant at being misunderstood, but respectful to God's leader. She explained her "bitterness of soul" and the vow she had made. Then Eli, as God's mouthpiece, accepted the "covenant" on God's behalf.

Then Eli answered and said, Go in peace: and the God of Israel grant thee thy petition that thou hast asked of him.

1 Samuel 1:17

Part of the conditions she had made on her part had been what was called "a Nazarite vow." That meant she had promised that her little boy would never have his hair cut, would never eat or drink certain things, and would be dedicated to the Lord all of his life.

Remember the story of Samson? His strength was associated with that vow. When his hair was cut, he had broken the conditions on his part, and God's condition of strength was no longer in effect. In Samson's case, the Lord had initiated the contract. (Judges 13:1-21.) In Samuel's case, his mother initiated the contract. She made a vow, and God answered it.

God honored His part by opening her womb, and before the next sacrifice time, she had her little boy. For several years, she did not accompany her husband and the family back to Shiloh. (1 Sam. 1:21-23.) She enjoyed her baby and would not go back until it was time to honor her conditions to the vow — turning him over to the service of the Lord.

When he was weaned, she took him up to the tabernacle. Children nursed longer then, so he probably was between three and five years old at that time. At any rate, she took along the required offerings as well. (1 Sam. 1:24,25.) Then she gave Samuel to Eli's service, dedicating the boy to God.

Apparently, after that, she only saw him once a year when her family came up to offer the annual sacrifice. Then she brought him a new linen tunic, "a little coat," each year. And the Lord blessed her in return for the gift of her son, and she had three more sons and two daughters. (1 Sam. 2:18-21.)

You may think, "But that's a story about people in the Old Testament. They lived differently than us. What does that have to do with me?"

It has to do with us, *because God does not change.* A vow is still a vow. God even now expects your word to be your bond. He still will honor a vow, if you keep your part of it. Being a "contract, or covenant breaker" is a very serious matter to God. He made certain in His Word that we would understand how seriously He takes this matter of giving your word by telling us how much He values His Word.

If we truly have made Him our Father, then we should be like Him. We should be trustworthy, speaking out only things in line with His will, thinking only on those things that are pure and of good report (Philip. 4:8), and making every possible effort to say only what we mean and mean what we say.

When you make a vow to God, that is a very serious matter. He will "take your word" that you mean it. And, if you do not mean it, you have trouble in your life. Making vows is such a serious matter that you should consider it carefully before you do.

> When thou vowest a vow unto God, defer not to pay it; for he hath no pleasure in fools: pay that which thou hast vowed.
>
> Better is it that thou shouldest not vow, than that thou shouldest vow and not pay.
>
> Suffer not thy mouth to cause thy flesh to sin; neither say thou before the angel, that it was an error: wherefore should God be angry at thy voice, and destroy the work of thine hands?
>
> For in the multitude of dreams and many words there are also divers vanities: but fear thou God.
>
> Ecclesiastes 5:4-7

A Vow Is a Promise

A *vow* is a promise. When you make a conditional or unconditional vow, God expects you to keep it. He honors your vow by meeting your conditions. Then He sits back and waits for you to meet the conditions you promised Him.

God said through Solomon in those verses in Ecclesiastes that He considers those who make vows and break them as "fools." His attitude about this could not be plainer than in those verses.

*If you make it, keep it.

*If you cannot keep it, do not make it.

*If you make a vow and do not keep it, you are a fool.

*And there is no point in telling the recording angel that you "made a mistake," that you "really did not mean it." Surely God does not expect you to keep that vow? Why, everyone says things all the time they do not mean. God does not, and He does not want His children to operate that way, either.

The position we hold in God today is higher than Adam's was. Adam had dominion over the work of God's hand. (Gen. 1:28.) We have dominion through Jesus at God's right hand, sitting on His throne. We are not laborers *for* God as Adam was in the garden east of Eden (Gen. 2:8,15), but laborers *with* God. (1 Cor. 3:9.) We "rule and reign" with Jesus. (2 Tim. 2:12.)

Have you ever noticed that, when Jesus told His disciples — and all of His followers after them — to go and preach the Gospel to the world, He did not tell them how to do it? He left the "how" up to us. That is why traditional religious-doctrine folks are always left behind in God's moves. They always operate by ancient methods, by the way God did it last time. They are hung up on a certain way that God is supposed to move.

However, God is always doing things in new ways. He is a present-tense God, not a past tense. Have you ever noticed that people are no longer riding in wagons? Now we have automobiles, and most people have no problem buying and using all the latest appliances. But when it comes to Jesus, many Christians still are hung up on some old worn-out way that was new and fresh in its time but no longer works today.

On the other hand, God's principles and character never change. He only varies the way He does things, but His new things will always be based on steadfast principles laid down in the beginning. A vow is still a vow. It is still a promise and only as good as your word.

It will be difficult to walk in the promises of God or receive His wealth, if He cannot trust your word. It would be funny if it were not so sad: Many Christians have no faith in the *whole* counsel of God, yet *their* words are the ones that cannot be trusted.

If you make a vow and do not keep it, Solomon said God would destroy the works of your hands. (Eccl. 5:6.) Covenant-breakers are in big trouble. One of the most marvelous things that can ever happen in your life is to get to the place where God counts you a friend whom He can trust, not just a minor child.

A friend is not someone to whom you can talk, but someone whom you can trust. God still is trying to get the trust of many of His children and trying to move them to the place where He can trust them. It is hard to walk in health or wealth, if you cannot trust the one on whom you are basing your belief.

Look at Job 22:22-28:

> Receive, I pray thee, the law from his mouth, and lay up his words in thine heart.
>
> If thou return to the Almighty, thou shalt be built up, thou shalt put away iniquity far from thy tabernacles.
>
> Then shalt thou lay up gold as dust, and the gold of Ophir as the stones of the brooks.
>
> Yea, the Almighty shall be thy defence, and thou shalt have plenty of silver.
>
> For then shalt thou have thy delight in the Almighty, and shalt lift up thy face unto God.
>
> Thou shalt make thy prayer (petition) unto him, and he shall hear thee, and thou shalt pay thy vows.
>
> Thou shalt also decree a thing, and it shall be established unto thee: and the light shall shine upon thy ways.

In verse 27, God said through Eliphaz the Temanite (the application was not right in Job's case, but the words were true) that if you petition Him, He will hear you — but you better pay your vows! If you do that, then the next verse shows you that is how you can walk in dominion.

God was saying, "When you pray to me and make vows, stick with them, fulfill your part, and you will have authority whereby you can decree things. And what you decree shall be established."

Decreeing is done with the mouth. When God sees your commitment to fulfill your verbal contract, then when you speak a thing, God said, "I will do it." Keeping your word affects whether or not God answers your prayer.

In Genesis 28:20-22, we read of a man named Jacob who camped at a place called Bethel (House of God) and made a vow to God.

Jacob said, "God, if You'll be with me, give me food and clothing, and bring me back safely to my Father's house, I promise to give You a tenth of everything You give me."

That was a *conditional* vow. Three chapters later, we read where an angel appeared to Jacob and said, "I remember that vow you made." That is why Jacob's Uncle Laban could not stop his prosperity although he kept changing his wages ten times. (Gen. 31:7.)

Because Jacob had kept his vow, the angel then showed him how to establish a decree, how to let Laban get the best of him and still prosper. (Gen. 31:11-13.)

Hasty, Ill-Considered Vows Are Unwise

Jacob's story is one of a man who changed from a trickster into one whose word was his bond, one who kept his word to God. We can see that God also kept His part of the contract with Jacob.

Now let's look at a classic example of a hasty, ill-considered vow, where the man who made it certainly wished he could have changed it. That story is found in Judges 11. A man named Jephthah said:

> **And Jephthah vowed a vow unto the Lord, and said, If thou shalt without fail deliver the children of Ammon into mine hands,**

> **Then it shall be, that whatsoever cometh forth of the doors of my house to meet me, when I return in peace from the children of Ammon, shall surely be the Lord's, and I will offer it up for a burnt offering.**
> **Judges 11:30,31**

Jephthah won the battle, as he had asked the Lord, and when he got home:

> . . . Behold, his daughter came out to meet him with timbrels and with dances: and she was his only child; beside her he had neither son nor daughter.
>
> And it came to pass, when he saw her, that he rent his clothes, and said, Alas, my daughter! thou hast brought me very low, and thou art one of them that trouble me: for *I have opened my mouth* unto the Lord, and I cannot go back.
>
> And she said unto him, My father, if thou hast opened thy mouth unto the Lord, do to me according to that which hath proceeded out of thy mouth; forasmuch as the Lord hath taken vengeance for thee of thine enemies, even of the children of Ammon.
>
> **Judges 11:34-36**

If you read the rest of the story, you will see that he did not offer her as a literal sacrifice, but that she was dedicated to the service of the Lord. She remained a virgin and had no children, and as she was his only child, that meant he had no descendants to carry on his name. (Judges 11: 36-40.) That was a pretty costly vow.

However, at least he kept his word. He did not act the fool and break his vow to God. Another verse says that, if you have made a vow to your own hurt, keep it anyway and trust God to turn things because you have kept your word. (Ps. 15:4.)

When I was reading this once, the Holy Spirit said to me, ''Did you notice the respect children had then for their parents? Did you notice the trust children placed in their parents?''

The same thing is true of Abraham and Isaac. How many sons would trust the father's word enough to get on the altar, be tied down, and actually lie under a knife — simply because the father had said a sacrifice would be provided? The real point, however, is that the fathers had to already have established their words with the children. The sons and daughters had to already *know* beyond the shadow of a doubt that daddy would do what he said.

If you want your children to grow up trusting God, teach them first that they can trust you. Do not break your word to them if you can help. You think because they are children that it does not matter. But their future relationship with God, their ability to trust Him and His Word, may ride on *your* word.

Children today feel very put upon if they have to do what you say. There is no such thing as a "democratic order" in Scripture, at least not of God's doing. Actually, the majority voted and got their way with Aaron over the golden calf episode. (Ex. 32:1.)

God's Kingdom is a theocracy. All the "classes that exist" are the Godhead and servants (the rest of us). There is no "majority rule." There is no voting on things. God says it, and that is the way it is! God is not the author of democracy. And when you have democracy in your home, you really have problems. When there is "democracy" in the church, the pastor has problems.

So if you are considering making a covenant with God over something, please remember this contract is more important, and with more serious consequences if it is broken, than one you will ever find on earth. Make it simple, and make it one you know you can keep. Then seek the mind of Christ on it, and make sure it is acceptable to Him.

If you make an unconditional vow, again be sure to keep it. Otherwise, you will be crying and wondering why your finances are being hurt, and somehow you are not able to keep the proceeds from the works of your hands.

Memorial Offerings

For an example of a memorial offering, look at the story of Cornelius in Acts 10.

> **He** (Cornelius) **saw in a vision evidently about the ninth hour of the day an angel of God coming in to him, and saying unto him, Cornelius.**
>
> **And when he looked on him, he was afraid, and said, What is it, Lord? And he said unto him, *Thy prayers and thine alms* (giving to the poor) are come up for a *memorial* before God.**
>
> **Acts 10:3,4**

Cornelius' offerings and giving to the poor had come before God as a *memorial,* and God sent an angel across his path to summon the Apostle Peter to bring him, his family, and friends the message of salvation.

If what you are bringing God does not cost you anything, it is not good enough for a memorial offering. The woman who bought the costly ointment to anoint Jesus' feet and then dried His feet with her hair brought a "memorial" offering. Jesus said what she had done would be spoken of as a memorial to her wherever the Gospel was preached. (Mark 14:9.)

Bring God something out of your need. A memorial offering must cost you something. However, remember it is not the offering that moves God so much as the faith.

You can move into a place where God is able to open His hand to you by making vows and memorial offerings. However, you had better make sure you come through on your end!

Now I want to take you to give you knowledge of something that will set you free in a lot of areas and make this business of giving and receiving a lot simpler. That is to learn how to live a lifestyle of worship.

10
Develop a Lifestyle of Worship

Let us talk about the fact that *obedience* is the highest form of worship. Obedience is a lifestyle, not something you do once in a while, but something you do all of the time. *Sacrifices* were something you did periodically. They were "works," not a lifestyle, a way of living every day twenty-four hours a day. Look at 1 Samuel 15:22:

> . . . Behold, to obey is better than sacrifice, and to hearken than the fat of rams.

When you are practicing a lifestyle of submission and yielding to the Spirit of God to obey Him no matter what, then everything you do becomes worship. The word *worship* in the Greek means "to lick the hand like a dog" in order to gain favor. All of us want to gain favor from God, and the thing that pleases Him more than anything is obedience.

I have found that when you operate in a realm of obedience towards God in the things He asks you to do, then you also operate in a realm of anointing that is awesome.

In the area of financing, in order to walk in the fullness of wealth on a continuous basis, there must be faithfulness in what you do. You cannot tithe today, decide not to next Sunday, and expect God to bless you. God looks for consistency in His people all of the time.

You say, "Well, I tried for six months."

You do not "try" God. You either are going to do it, or you are not going to. Tithes and offerings are not something you try. They are the right things to do, because God said so. Choose anything else but what He has said, and you are into rebellion. Samuel told Saul how serious rebellion is:

> **For rebellion is as the sin of witchcraft, and stubbornness is as iniquity and idolatry. Because thou hast rejected the word of the Lord, he hath also rejected thee from being king.**
> **1 Samuel 15:23**

Christians need to make sure they are doing everything they know to do, everything God has told them. That is called *faithfulness.* Proverbs 28:20 says that the man who is faithful **shall abound with blessings,** but the person who sets out to get rich at all costs will not be innocent. In other words, normally you cannot get rich quick without in some way being into sin.

God says the kind of person who is faithful is the one who is going to be bountifully (richly) blessed. If God cannot trust you to give a dime out of a dollar, how can He trust you to give a hundred dollars out of a thousand?

Earlier, I wrote briefly about the testing my wife and I went through when we made a vow to give God twenty percent of our income. My vow was not wiped out because I started operating in lack, or because we wanted to buy something new. Faithfulness in maintaining that vow was top priority in our budget and still is.

Do not let circumstances dictate whether you give or do not give. Keep on giving, if you want to receive all of the time. The Bible says if you give freely, you receive freely. (Matt. 10:8.) If you have given good offerings to anointed men and women of God, you cannot help but be blessed.

If you just began tithing and giving, you need to remember there is a period between "seed time" and "harvest." In between is the period where faithfulness counts, a lifestyle of obedience that amounts to worship of God.

God said in Genesis 8:22 that as long as the earth remains, seedtime and harvest will continue. He was talking about the seasons, of course. Nevertheless, the same principles apply in all areas. As long as the earth remains, God's ways of blessing His people remain the same.

Make a lifestyle of planting. Plant in the morning, and plant in the evening. Keep planting. Once you understand that God cannot lie, once you have that settled in your thinking, then you can *stand* in patience and wait for your "bread" to return to you on the waters.

Sow in the morning and in the evening, because you do not know which one is going to come up. Once seed is planted, it is out of your hands. You have no control over when it comes up nor how much. That is why in Matthew 13:8, Jesus said:

> **But other fell into good ground, and brought forth fruit, some an hundredfold, some sixtyfold, some thirtyfold.**

Only God knows what the return will be. When you put a seed into the ground, you are trusting the soil and God to give you back more than you have planted. However, *once it is planted,* it is out of your hands.

Jesus told a parable about a man who planted seed, and *while he slept,* an enemy sowed weeds in his crop. The point is that the man did not stay in his field every day, poking around his seed to see if it was growing. He went to bed and got up and went to bed and got up. In other words, day followed day until the harvest, which comes at the proper time. When is the proper time? When the fruit has ripened.

Move Quickly at Harvest Time

Not long ago, my church seemed to go from twenty miles an hour to two hundred and forty! I have no idea which seed the harvest came from. I do not know how long ago that seed had been planted. We just looked at the "signs" of abundance one day and realized the harvest was in.

When we recognized the harvest, we put the sickle in quickly. You have to move quickly when the harvest is ready, or you lose the crop. You cannot sit around and wonder whether or not it is going to rain. (Eccl. 11:3,4.) We reaped a bus, a studio of camera equipment, and some other things.

When the door opens — move! Do not sit around wondering whether you should or should not. Move! We spend too much time sometimes worrying, "Is it God, or is it not?" As I wrote in the last chapter, you better spend quiet time learning to hear the voice of God for yourself, so that you will know when it is time to move and not have to wonder.

Many people miss the blessings of God because they do not know His timing nor hear His voice. God help the Church for its basic insensitivity to the Holy Spirit! I live a lifestyle of listening to His voice. I know when God is "bringing in the sheaves" for some corn that has been planted. I can sense it every time when the door pops open.

God is continuing to bring in a harvest for us. As I preached this series and prepared for this book, things kept happening for us every day. I did not decide it was time to move into television — God did. He made His timing clear by providing what we needed to accomplish His purpose.

I do not mean to imply that everything has been "peaches and cream" since then. The devil is angry. He has tried to attack the equipment from all kinds of angles. If you are doing something for God, you *will* suffer tribulation. (John 16:33.) You simply have to get up, run the devil off, and start again. That is part of faithfulness.

Receiving a harvest requires patience. Solomon wrote in Ecclesiastes 7:8 that **Better is the end of a thing than the beginning thereof.** If you plant seed, the better end of that is the harvest. The rest of that verse says that the patient in spirit is better than the proud in spirit.

Your business is planting; God's business is bringing the harvest. You take care of your part, and let God take care of His. Also, your business is gathering in the harvest. I cannot advise you too strongly not to sit around thinking you will get to it next week. If you put off moving to gather in the harvest, what could happen? The rains and storms could come and destroy the fruit on the vine.

God has no use for lazy people, and I am afraid there are a lot of lazy people today in the Body of Christ. Jesus told a story of a landowner who gave more to his steward who had increased what was given him in the beginning. And he took away from the servant with no increase what he already had. (Matt. 25:15-28.)

The man who got more was faithful and industrious about his master's business. The man who buried his money was lazy and lost everything. God called working people, not lazy people. God really instituted what we call "the work ethic" in the Garden of Eden. Adam's work was easy compared to the kind of work that came on the earth after the fall. (Gen. 3:17-19,23.) Nevertheless, God had set work for Adam to do looking after the garden and the animals. (Gen. 2:15.)

We were created to work six days and rest one. (Ex. 20:9.) If you think that is Old Testament, look at Hebrews 6:12:

> **That ye be not slothful, but followers of them who through faith and patience inherit the promises.**

Also, as I mentioned before, Paul's advice in an epistle to the Thessalonians was that "those who do not work should not eat." (2 Thess. 3:10.) The reason Paul wrote this was because he knew idle people get into trouble. He had heard that some among the Thessalonian church were "disorderly," did not work at all, and were "busybodies." (v. 11.)

You can see from that verse that the three things go together: *industriousness* (planting seeds), *faith* (believing they will bring a harvest), and *patience* (waiting for God's timing). God demands patience from us. In order to receive the harvest, He does not ask for patience as an option. He demands it. He is not moved if you worry. He is not moved by anxiety, cares, and burdens. He only is moved by faith.

He is not even moved by *need*. If He were moved by our needs, none of us would have any. In that case, however, we would never develop trust and faith in our Father, nor would we ever mature. We would be like babies being handed bottles and pacifiers. So your needs do not impress God, although I know the Holy Spirit is sorrowful to see His people going without when they could easily have their needs met.

God set in motion a pattern for us that would bring maturity, a way in which He could more than meet our needs, a way in which He could give us abundantly over our needs. However, He *knew* what it would take to get us to grow up spiritually. That is faith and faithfulness, which together make up willing obedience.

Jesus patiently endured the things He experienced on earth, and He obtained the promise. (Heb. 6:15.) We can do the same. Jesus "planted" seeds in the disciples and received more than a hundredfold of souls. We are not told that He gave alms and tithes. However, we can be sure He did, because His parents made the proper sacrifices (Luke 2:21-39,42-51), and so did everyone in the society of the day. He was careful to do all according to the law, **to fulfill all righteousness** (Matt. 3:14,15).

There is no way He did not "practice" what He preached. If He found that necessary for willing obedience, how much more should we? Hebrews 10:35,36 says:

> **Cast not away therefore your confidence, which hath great recompence of reward.**
>
> **For ye have need of patience, that, after ye have done the will of God, ye might receive the promise.**

The context of those verses was some persecution those people had gone through and a reminder of their eternal rewards to come; however, the principles are just as true of short-term harvests in this life.

First John 5:14,15 says:

> And this is the confidence that we have in him, that, if we ask any thing according to his will, he heareth us:
>
> And if we know that he hear us, whatsoever we ask, we know that we have the petitions that we desired of him.

When you ask according to His Word, you can be bold. That is why I go around boldly declaring things. That is why I always talk "abundance." Every time I talk about finances, I declare bold things. My first obligation is to please God and do the work of the ministry.

Respect Is Part of Worship

In a previous chapter, I wrote about the importance of respect for God's offices in the Body and the effect disrespect could have on your finances. Dishonor and disrespect cause God's hand to close over you. If you wonder why your harvest has been delayed, my advice would be to examine closely your attitudes toward things of God and people of God — not just the five-fold offices, but the brothers and sisters around you.

The Lord spoke to me one day about this in a really shocking manner.

He said, "My people are rude. They are rude to Me and rude to each other."

Here is a "checklist" for attitudes of disrespect:

*Do you come in church whispering and laughing, visiting back and forth while the service is going on?

*Do you think when the ministry of the gifts begins that it signals "bathroom break"?

*Do you joke and make fun of the pastor or his wife, or any other leaders in the church?

*Do you criticize, judge, and make jokes about televangelists? Not all of them are doing everything perfectly. Not all of them even are living right, as we have found out to our sorrow in the last few years. However, *that is God's business*, not ours.

He said, "Who are you to criticize another man's servant?" (Rom. 14:4.)

They are *His* servants and our brothers and sisters. More than that, they are our leaders. If David knew enough to honor and be respectful of Saul, who was trying to kill him, surely we ought to have enough spiritual sense not to judge and criticize even fallen leaders. They are still "the called of God" and anointed according to His purposes.

If you want your harvest not to be aborted, be very careful *not to touch God's anointed*. (1 Chron. 16:22.) As I wrote earlier, if you are in a position where you feel it is right for you to bring something to the attention of a ministry office, then do it in a right and respectful manner and only after "praying it through."

*Do you crack jokes and indulge in loud talk and laughter during choir practice when the director is trying to bring a disciplined and anointed sound forth for the services?

*Do you get up and move around during an altar call?

God told me the people in my church were rude.

He said, "Deal with it! When Moses came before Me out in the desert, I demanded that He take off His shoes because he was standing on holy ground. The priests had to stop and wash themselves before coming into My presence in the tabernacle and the temple.''

If the priests did not honor this, they would have died instantly. God is holy. As the Creator, the One who owns us, and our Father, He deserves respect. If you would stand up in the presence of the President of the United States, what more should you do for God?

As usual, God's ways are opposite. When Jesus has appeared to people, and when the presence of the Holy Spirit is heavy, people usually cannot stand up. They fall prostrate instead.

The point is: Examine your attitude to God and the things of God. Repent if you have been disrespectful, and change your attitudes and your behavior. I promise you that will have an effect upon your finances.

One of the major pastor-evangelists, who holds large crusades, already is operating to straighten out this disorder in the Body. In his church, he could care less about *your* feelings, if they come in conflict with God's.

He says very plainly, ''I do not want any fleshly manifestations. I do not want any moving around. If you cannot be quiet and respectful, you will be ushered politely out.''

When we are rude to the place God has ordained us to meet, it is the same as being rude to Him.

When we are rude to the people God has set over us in the Body, it is the same as being rude to the Holy Spirit.

Since the Lord spoke to me, I have set my church in order. I demand respect for what is going on in the church, because I am responsible for the knowledge that has been given me. I also am responsible for the place God has given us to meet. My ushers have been instructed that if the people present during a service do not conform to the guidelines of respect that have been set up, they are to escort those people out of the church.

God holds me accountable, so if I am in the middle of my message, and I hear whispering or a commotion somewhere, I stop and say, "Please be quiet over on that side."

The first time, I am polite and do not call names. But if the disturbance persists, I will point to the person or persons and call them down. We even insist that children do not make unnecessary trips to the bathroom.

Actually, when I was growing up, the attitude of respect was much better than now.

My mother used to say, "Use the bathroom now, before you leave home. Because you will *not* get up during the service to go to the bathroom."

You may think I, and the others to whom God has spoken about the prevalent rudeness in the Body, am being too hard. You may even think we are being rude and harsh to the people, even to the point of embarrassing them. However, people's feelings do not matter alongside God's feelings. And this is a much more serious matter than you might think.

God specifically said to me, "I am not going to do much until I get respect."

So if we want God to move again in our midst in a full way as He did in past revivals, we had better "get our acts together" and begin to give Him the proper respect.

11

As You Think, So Are You

If you are not prospering in your soul and in your inner man, it is going to be hard to prosper on the outside. The Bible says that, "as a man thinketh in his heart, so is he." (Prov. 23:7.) You can be giving tithes and giving offerings, but if you have a poverty mentality, if you think God hates prosperity and wants us to have just enough to pay our bills, the blessings will not come upon you.

If you think God only wants us to have enough to get by, you have missed the whole Bible. God's declaration throughout His Word is that His desire is for His people to have abundance in their lives. It is "warped" thinking to believe that God walks around on streets of gold (*made* of gold, not *paved* with gold), but wants us to barely get along.

When I look at the people who obeyed God in the Bible, I see people who walked in tremendous prosperity. Abraham was not broke. David and Solomon were not poor. After the devil tested Job, God restored twice as much as he had before (Job 42:10), and the brother was not living "shabbily" to begin with!

God told Isaac to sow in famine. Nothing was happening, and the "economy" around him was dead.

However, God told him not to go down to Egypt as his father had done in times of famine.

"Stay where I tell you, and plant something," God said. (Gen. 26:1-6.)

I am sure the people around Isaac thought he was crazy. There had been no rain, and the ground must have been hard as a rock. Yet he went out there with his servants and began to dig. When God speaks, His word supersedes all other natural laws. Isaac received a great harvest, a hundred times as much as he planted. (Gen. 26:12.)

If God is going to put us up in mansions, He does not want us to have log-cabin mentalities. The God I serve is not broke, nor is He the creator of poverty.

Let's look at one of the "blessings" chapters in order for you to get it fixed firmly in your mind that God wants His people prosperous. If you can begin to think that way instead of expecting poverty, you will see your circumstances change.

> The Lord shall establish thee an holy people unto himself, as he hath sworn unto thee, if thou *shalt keep the commandments* of the Lord thy God, *and walk in his ways.*
>
> And all people of the earth shall see that thou art called by the name of the Lord; (I wrote earlier that God showed me this is one of His primary purposes for blessing His people — for the world to see we have a *real* God) and they shall be afraid of thee.

The strategic verses follow *obedience:*

> And the Lord shall make thee plenteous in goods, in the fruit of thy body, and in the fruit of thy ground, in the land which the Lord sware unto thy fathers to give thee.
>
> The Lord shall open unto thee his good treasure, the heaven to give rain unto thy land in his season,

and to bless the work of thine hand: and thou shalt
lend unto many nations, and thou shalt not borrow.

And the Lord shall make thee the head, and not
the tail; and thou shalt be above only, and thou shalt
not be beneath; if that thou hearken unto the
commandments of the Lord thy God, which I
command thee this day to observe and to do them.
Deuteronomy 28:9-13

At the beginning of that chapter, God said the
blessings would overtake them *if they listened to His
voice.* As we have already seen that God does not
change, as His people, we can expect the same
blessings today — *if we listen to His voice and do His
commandments.* If you are thinking poverty, depression,
and hard times, you are not listening to His voice.

To obey you must hear intelligently. You must give
attention to His voice. Other definitions are "to consent
to" His voice, "to discern" His voice, "to give ear to,"
and "to be obedient to understand" His voice. That
is the condition to having prosperity and walking in
dominion.

Talk about having dominion! We are supposed to
be on top calling the shots. That is "kingdom rule."
Dominion is an awesome word. It means "to rule" or
"the power to rule." God always meant for His people
to have the power to rule over circumstances and their
surroundings. We should be ruling over the economy,
not the economy ruling over us.

The "Doer" Gets Blessed

It is not the one who talks that gets blessed; it is
not even the one who believes. It is the person who
"does" the commandments of God who gets blessed.
Those commandments include giving tithes, giving
offerings, walking in the way of the Lord (right

attitudes), *and* having faith that God's promises are true. In other words, *believing* that you will receive what He has promised when you meet the conditions.

In Matthew, Jesus said the one who *hears* and *does* is like a man who builds his house on a rock instead of sand. (Matt. 7:24,25.) He also said:

> For a good tree bringeth not forth corrupt fruit; neither doth a corrupt tree bring forth good fruit.
>
> For every tree is known by his own fruit. For of thorns men do not gather figs, nor of a bramble bush gather they grapes.
>
> A good man out of the treasure of his heart bringeth forth that which is good; and an evil man out of the evil treasure of his heart bringeth forth that which is evil: for of the abundance of the heart his mouth speaketh.
>
> Luke 6:43-46

The "abundance of the heart" is whatever you think. If you do not *think* God will bless you, all of your giving is not really doing any good, because it must be from a cheerful, willing heart to truly be in line with His Word. Giving from religious, traditional, or other wrong motives means you have *wrong thinking.*

In order to be a true "doer," you must be a "right thinker." You must think in line with the Word of God.

Perhaps you are thinking that you have not given tithes and have not given offerings because you did not understand all of the principles you have read in this book. Perhaps you are wishing you had known them years ago and wondering how many blessings you have lost because of wrong thinking.

I have good news for you. Look at Job: When he got his thinking about God straightened out (Job 42:1-6) and repented, God restored twice as much as he originally had. When you turn back to God and do the right thing, He will return your loss to you. Some of you lost your things because you were disobeying the Lord. Return and obey the voice of the Lord, and He will make you abundantly prosperous in every work of your hand. (Deut. 30:8.)

Perhaps the most concise verse along this line is Isaiah 1:19:

If ye be willing and obedient, ye shall eat the good of the land.

You cannot repent, however, if you do not see that you *need* to repent. If the material and scriptures in this book do not convince you that poverty is not spiritual and that your Father in Heaven wishes you to prosper and have abundance, please search the Word of God for yourself.

Of course, you need to be able to hear God for yourself on this and other matters. Not just in prayer time, but in your car and anywhere you are, you ought to be able to tune in to the Holy Spirit.

Just say, "Hello, my Friend. Just wanted to say 'Hi' to You."

When you get the fellowship going in your relationship with God, boldness comes; blessed assurance comes. Part of the reason why many Christians do not "hear" the Holy Spirit is that they will not be still long enough.

God said, **Be still, and know that I am God** (Ps. 46:10).

If you feel guilty when you are not saying anything during your prayer time, that is another kind of "wrong thinking" that needs to be changed. That is the way you were trained. However, if you talked all the time to another person and never waited, or listened, for his reply, how long would that person stay around you?

Sometimes I go into prayer time and get ready for worship, and the Holy Spirit will say, "No, listen." Tradition would make you feel guilty for not worshipping. God is not a God of routine, although He is a God of decency and order. However, "order" does not always have to be carried out the same way.

God is sovereign. If He wants you to do nothing but sit one day — then sit!

If tomorrow He says, worship Me the whole time, just worship.

If He says, "Read My Word," then read.

Do not box Him in to a certain format. He looks at the heart, not at routines, programs, and activities.

Many times when the enemy tries to whisper to me, "You didn't get in x-amount of time at this or that," the Spirit of God will say, "Don't box Me in. I'm sovereign. I can do what I want to do. I know you, and I have seen your heart."

Sometimes I have experienced a greater anointing when I have simply spent time listening in His presence and did not have time to worship. The anointing seems to just drop on me.

In some services, the greatest moves of God happen when nothing seems to be going on. The Spirit will witness to you to be quiet, and all of a sudden, He moves. God likes "star time." He is the Superstar. When everyone is quiet in a church service, most of them are thinking of Him (if they have been trained to expect this). Then He has center stage, and when He has center stage, He can act. All of a sudden miracles begin to happen.

If we want His presence to be the main attraction, then we must have the atmosphere conducive to His presence, in church and in private. I have found that when we have a reverence for His presence through quietness and order, then we do not grieve Him, and He can move sovereignly. I like services where I do not control but the Holy Spirit does.

You Will Speak as You Think

Another reason why it is so important to straighten out your thinking is that you will speak out what you think. Not only your actions but your speech is governed by the mind, and if the mind is not governed by the spirit — the real you — then your actions and your talk will not be in line with the Holy Spirit.

James wrote that the tongue is full of deadly poison, and that the power of life and death is in the tongue. He also wrote about how hard it is to "bridle" the tongue. Some people need horses' bridles on their tongues! They need to be saying "Whoa!" not "Giddy up" to their tongues.

> **For in many things we offend all. If any man offend not in word, the same is a perfect man, and able also to bridle the whole body.**
>
> **Behold, we put bits in the horses' mouths, that they may obey us; and we turn about their whole body.**
>
> **Behold also the ships, which though they be so great, and are driven of fierce winds, yet are they turned about with a very small helm, whithersoever the governor listeth.**
>
> **Even so the tongue is a little member, and boasteth great things. Behold, how great a matter a little fire kindleth!**

> **And the tongue is a fire, a world of iniquity: so
> is the tongue among our members, that it defileth the
> whole body, and setteth on fire the course of nature;
> and it is set on fire of hell.**
>
> **For every kind of beasts, and of birds, and of
> serpents, and of things in the sea, is tamed, and hath
> been tamed of mankind:**
>
> **But the tongue can no man tame; it is an unruly
> evil, full of deadly poison.**
>
> James 3:2-8

You would not have nearly as many problems in
life if you learned how to control your tongue. Some
of you talk yourself into sickness, out of marriage, out
of good jobs, and out of wealth. Let only positive
things, good things in line with God's will, come out
of your mouth. However, you must really *believe* those
things, or the words are without power.

Therefore, you can see how important it is to get
your thinking lined up with God's Word.

Walking in dominion (the authority of Jesus'
name) depends on your believing that you have the
right and that you can do that. God gave Adam
dominion over the works of His hands (Gen. 1:28), and
those works include the heavenlies. Did you know that
God formed the stars and the moon by His finger? (Ps.
8:3.) The things in the heavenlies are also "the works
of God's hand."

When Satan tricked Eve, and Adam agreed with
her instead of God, man lost the dominion. Satan
became the ruler of the world's systems. But Jesus, the
second Man, *destroyed* the works of Satan (1 John 3:8),
and gave the authority and dominion to His Body.

However, the reason the devil could go back and forth from the heavenlies to the earth and make his headquarters there is because he also had dominion there as well as on earth. All of the earth and the heavens are "the works of God's hands."

The devil is still operating on earth and in the heavenlies *because we have not exercised our authority and run him out.* He already is defeated. You have been given all power over all of his power. (Matt. 28:18-20.) Yet, somehow, the Church has been acting for most of the last two thousand years as if the devil still had legal authority, and we were defeated!

Joshua used his tongue to decree that the sun and moon stop while he finished defeating his enemies. (Josh. 10:12-14.) He decreed it, and God established it. Joshua took dominion over the heavenlies.

Learn to use your tongue to take dominion over your circumstances, your surroundings, and your finances. God will back you up. Jesus has defeated the devil and destroyed his works. We are fighting an already defeated foe, and we have weapons and power much stronger than his.

Get your thinking straight: *You* are to take dominion. Do not let the enemy deceive you into thinking you cannot win. You already have won! Poverty, sickness, and sin belong to the devil. They are not part of God's plan for you. He plans prosperity, health, and righteous living for you. All you have to do is believe it, receive it, and walk in it.

If your words have doubt and disbelief, that comes out of your mind, and you will kill your blessings. If your words are flaky, they come out of "flaky thinking." God will not bless flakiness (presumption and weirdness). Also, if you attack, judge, criticize, gossip, and lie about (or to) your brothers and sisters in Christ, your words reflect your thinking.

When the Lord appeared to Saul on the road to Damascus, He said, "Why are you persecuting Me?" Saul never persecuted Jesus in the natural, but he was persecuting the followers of Christ. Jesus was saying, "When you come against them, you come against Me." The same thing is true today.

You may say, "But I don't persecute Christians!"

Do you talk about them? Do you judge others and, especially, the leaders? Do you gossip and lie about other Christians? If so, then you are "persecuting" the brethren.

We live in a sad society today. America is in a post-Christian mode, so we need to exercise dominion more than ever before in this country. Many of us have found that we cannot even trust the word of our brothers in Christ. It is sad when you must have legal contracts between Christians.

Remember the days when your parents or grandparents simply shook hands on a bargain, because *their words were their bonds?* Bank loans were made on a handshake and a promise. Even in the Christian community today, many of our words are not worth anything.

And, if that is the case, how can your words exercise rightful dominion over your circumstances? If the devil knows your words do not mean anything, he will not pay any attention to what you say.

12

An Exchange of Wealth Is About to Take Place

The wealth that God says belongs to Him and that was restored to the dominion of His people through Jesus still remains in a few people's hands. All most of them do with it is pile it up in banks, invest it to make more, live luxuriously on it, or use it as power over others. It is not being used to preach the Gospel and get souls saved. Those people are stockpiling it for themselves.

The media keeps talking about shortages. However, there really are no shortages in the earth. The earth's resources are so abundant that we could supply everyone. God would not have created a planet with lack. He created the earth with abundance of resources, enough to take care of every human being ever to be born.

Yet we live in economic false security even in the best of times. Why is that? Why does the sinner still have the majority of wealth, although it has been back under the stewardship of God's people for about two thousand years?

The reason is that the Church of Jesus Christ does not walk in the fullness of what they have been given dominion over, because of lack of knowledge.

However, for the past two decades, the knowledge that God not only designed but desires His people to prosper has begun to permeate the Church.

The command to "be fruitful, multiply, replenish and subdue, and take dominion" over the earth has been restored to many Christians as a truth of God. Basically, that four-fold command is the "prime directive" for mankind.

I believe that we are approaching the time when the wealth is to be restored sovereignly to the dominion of the Church.

God said to me, "I released the wealth back to My people when My Son came to earth."

He asked me, "Do you realize that originally all the wealth in the world was under the stewardship of Adam?"

When Lucifer tricked Eve, and Adam knowingly gave up dominion, the wealth was transferred to the rulership of Satan. Man lost control of the earth's wealth and resources. Then along came Jesus, who restored ownership and stewardship back to God's family.

Before too much longer, I believe we are going to see an exchange of wealth take place. The people who will benefit from that exchange are *the ones walking now in obedience* toward God's Word. Not every Christian will benefit. If you are not doing the right thing now with little, you cannot expect God to bless you with much.

God looks for good stewardship. You must prove to Him over a season of time that you are not a Christian simply to get the blessings, but because you love Him. If all you are tithing and planting seeds for is to get money, then your motives are wrong. You are planting "bad seed."

Giving is a lifestyle, as I wrote earlier, not something you decide to do once in a while. You do it because it is the normal thing for a Christian to do.

Just as worship should be a lifestyle, obedience should be a lifestyle, faith also should be a lifestyle. That should be the way you live, twenty-four hours a day. You should not have to stop and pray to "work up" faith. Faith ought to flow out of you automatically all the time.

However, it does take time to move into that kind of lifestyle. But, if you never start, and if you are not consistent with it, you never develop a lifestyle of conforming to the image of Jesus. (Rom. 8:29.) You need to set your eyes so on God that you walk as Jesus did all of the time. That means doing nothing of your own will but only what pleases the Father. Jesus did not "do His own thing." He only did what the Father said.

> **Then answered Jesus and said unto them, Verily, verily, I say unto you, The Son can do nothing of himself, but what he seeth the Father do: for what things soever he doeth, these also doeth the Son likewise.**
>
> **For the Father loveth the Son, and sheweth him all things that himself doeth: and he will shew him greater works than these, that ye may marvel.**
>
> **John 5:19,20**

God keeps saying to me, "Worship is not simply a prescribed time you set aside to say, 'Lord, I love you.' It is a lifestyle of obedience to Me. That is worship."

He said, "Let Me share this truth about My Son. People have a deception in their minds that when Jesus went aside to pray, He was simply doing a lot of talking to Me. However, if you read the Scripture, you will find that what He did was come into My presence and find out what I wanted Him to do. Then He went out of My presence and did those things. After that, He came back and listened some more.''

I have found the only way I can relax is to go into the presence of God, and be still. In those moments, God begins to speak to my heart and show me the things He desires me to do. When I go out and do them, that is worship.

Also, I can be in my car, when all of a sudden, God prompts worship and praise to come out of my mouth. If praise is in your heart, it will sometimes just gush out toward God. It will not be something you make up, contrive, or think you ought to say. It will come from your spirit and flow out your mouth. It will be easy. In the meantime, your daily walk speaks of worship to God.

The wealth of the sinner is going to change hands, but you will not benefit from that, if you are not doing the right thing.

God wants you to benefit from the wealth He already has placed in the earth. He takes pleasure in your prospering. He wants you to prosper, but you want to have right priorities. You must keep everything in order:

Give God His, minister to the needy, and enjoy what is left.

Always remember that the purpose of wealth is to fulfill God's plans, not your pocket. In fulfilling His purpose, God will make sure you have enough left over for yourself.

Do Not Be Jealous of Wealthy Sinners

I want to show you a wealth exchange in the Bible. In Exodus, we see the first time God took wealth from the sinner and gave it to the just (Prov. 13:22), as a corporate action. He had blessed people before that with abundance, people such as Abraham, Job, and others. But this time, He transferred wealth wholesale from one group to another.

First I want to give you a warning: Whatever you do, do not become jealous of the sinner who is prospering. Do not become envious. Try to get him saved, and do not desire to get him saved just to get his money!

Money is neutral. In itself, it is neither good nor bad. The threefold purpose of wealth we have talked about before. If money is not being used for those three things, it is being used in an ungodly way. However, the use to which money is put depends on the one who has it. If the wealthy sinner gets saved, then so does his money! At least, hopefully, he will use it for God's purposes after that.

There are some unbelievers, however, who make up their minds not to change. And when God gets ready to transfer wealth, they are going to lose theirs.

I am talking about the transfer of wealth from the Egyptians, who refused to change and honor God, to the Israelites. (Ex. 11:2,3.) The Bible says **the Lord gave the people favour in the sight of the Egyptians** (v. 3), so that they gave them jewels of silver and jewels of gold. That is how the Lord transferred the wealth, by causing the Egyptians to have favour toward Israel and want to give them wealth.

Also, the Word says that the Egyptian people looked up to Moses, especially the king's servants. (v. 3.) They saw the great things he did on behalf of the Lord.

Then, when they took possession of the land promised to Abraham's descendants, God transferred the land with its cities, vineyards, and other wealth from "the Kenites, the Kenizzites, the Kadmonites, the Hittites, the Perizzites, the Rephaims, the Amorites, the Canaanites, the Girgasites, and the Jebusites" (Gen. 15:18-21) and gave it to Israel, from the River of Egypt to the Euphrates.

God transferred the wealth from sinners to His saints. *God* did the transfer. He said, "I am going to take this land from them and give it to you." (v. 18.)

Favor follows God's people. Abraham walked in favor wherever he went, because Abraham lived a lifestyle of worship (obedience and willing faithfulness). So did Abraham's offspring — as long as they kept their part of the covenant — to hear and obey.

What you do will affect your offspring. As parents, you have a great responsibility to teach your children the right things so that they can benefit from what you have done. What you are doing now determines whether you and your children have favor later with God.

I have heard people teach that the Church does not want money from drug dealers, beer companies, prostitution, and gambling. But money in itself is not sinful. Of course, you cannot indulge in those sins and try to salve your conscience by giving the money. In that case, the money would not be acceptable to God because of *your* motives.

However, if God moves on a sinner to donate money to His causes, there is nothing wrong with the money. God built His first tabernacle from the silver and gold that came from people who worshipped idols. In Nehemiah, we see where a Gentile king financed the rebuilding of the temple when the Jewish people returned from exile. (Neh. 3.)

God can take an unsaved source and use it to finance His projects. Once the money changes hands, *the purpose has changed.* Money does not have a conscience. It is simply a tool used in the earth to establish God's covenant, as it is in Heaven.

Ecclesiastes 10:9 says that money answers all things. It can be used for good or bad. If a drug dealer wanted to give me a million dollars, I would take it, and pray for the brother's salvation. I would try to get him saved. The moment that money touched my hands, its purpose would have been changed. It would have been the "wealth of the wicked" being transferred to the just.

Money is money. As long as no strings are attached, a sinner's money is as good for the Kingdom as yours. God has let me know that He is going to permit the unsaved to do a lot of the financing of my ministry.

This is why it is important to treat everyone right. The Bible says you might entertain an angel unawares, when you entertain strangers. Do good to all men. Walk in peace with all, as much as is possible. You never know when you might walk into a sinner whom God had been dealing with to put a hundred thousand dollars in your hand for the work of God.

Look at what Job said, during the time he was trying to sort out what had happened to him:

This is the portion of a wicked man with God, and the heritage of oppressors, which they shall receive of the Almighty.

If his children be multiplied, it is for the sword: and his offspring shall not be satisfied with bread.

Though he heap up silver as the dust, and prepare raiment as the clay:

He may prepare it, *but the just shall put it on, and the innocent shall divide the silver.*

Job 27:13,14,16,17

The sinner will work and work to pile up all that wealth, and God will suddenly say, "I'll pull a switch on this. I will let My people benefit from it. The innocent will divide all this silver."

The wealth exchange can take place just like that. You may be going along broke, barely having enough to make your tithes and offerings. But then God transfers some wealth from a sinner, and your harvest has come in.

I believe God is setting His people up for this wealth exchange.

To be ready for this exchange, we *must* change our thinking. We must stop thinking, talking, and walking "defeated." We must stop expecting to be poor. We need to study what happened with one of the judges of Israel named Gideon.

The Church must have a core of "Gideons" to be able to do what God wants done with the wealth He transfers. The entire Body of Christ does not have to be in a spiritual position to take all of the territory God wants taken. However, there will have to be a "Gideon generation," a remnant who can follow orders and be faithful.

13

The Gideon Generation

In order to be ready for the exchange of wealth, we must be "trend setters." We must be the ones who do things differently than the crowd. We must not think like the world, or even as traditional churches do in our day. We must think the way God does for our time.

Look at the story of Gideon. He was a nobody, from one of the less well-known and poorest families in the tribe of Manasseh. When the angel of the Lord appeared to Gideon and called him "a mighty man of valor" (Judges 6:12), Gideon must have thought the angel had really missed it!

He said, "What are you talking about? My family is among the poorest in the tribe, and I am the least in my family! Besides, if the Lord is with us, why are we having so much trouble? It looks to me as if He has forsaken us into the hands of our enemies." (Judges 6:12-15.)

However, the angel prevailed, although the Lord had to do a couple of miracles before Gideon was confident enough to move out for Him. When he did take hold of the Lord's will, he really moved. He began by tearing down an altar to Baal and building an altar to the Lord on top of it. That was a pretty brave thing to do, considering his standing in the community.

When the Lord was ready for him to go into battle, God said a strange thing. He said:

"You have too *many* people with you to win this war." (Judges 7:2.)

Did you ever hear of a commander-in-chief who thought he had too many soldiers? God's concern was that Israel would think they had won the battle themselves. He does not want you ever to forget that He is God. He is sovereign, and He lets us help in order to give us a part in what He is doing. But He could do it without us, obviously.

So He kept cutting down the size of Gideon's army, until it reached only three hundred men. Also, God chose those men because they drank their water differently than the others. (Judges 7:5-7.) These three hundred certainly had a different way of fighting, as well. They used trumpets and lights hidden under pitchers.

When they suddenly broke the pitchers — so that all of their lights shone into the enemy's camp in the middle of the night — and blew the trumpets loudly, most of their enemies were so scared that they **ran, and cried, and fled** (v.21).

The point is that God does not want us ever to forget who wins the battles and who gets the credit. He is looking for a remnant of the Church today who will be willing to hear Him and willing to take the territory in unorthodox ways, if He says to.

Part of the blessings of the covenant are for God to make your foes flee from you. (Ex. 15:16,23:27; Deut. 2:25.)

In this move of God, we also will "fight" differently than in previous moves. Because God had

"Gideon's Three Hundred" use trumpets and lights under pitchers does not mean that marching around the walls seven days, as they did at Jericho, was wrong. It only means that God uses different methods at different times.

However, His principles do not change. The principles of warfare are like everything else of God: Hear and obey Him, and you *will* win the battle. If you are trying to win this battle in some way simply because that way worked last time, you are not hearing God.

On the other hand, if you begin to think that the way He gave you the battle *this* time is a better way than the way He had your parents win, then you are in danger of pride. You will find yourself holding onto "your" method when God has moved on to yet a different way.

So do not get "hung up" on old moves, previous battles. What happened yesterday was God's will for yesterday. But that was yesterday. Let's go on and see what God has for today. Do you like stale bread? You can go into some old, established churches and smell mold instead of fresh bread.

God says, "I am fresh. I am new every day. There is no time with Me. All things are 'present' tense with Me."

The Lord told Israel when they were ready to enter the promised land that their part was only to be strong and courageous so that they might do everything according to His direction through Joshua. (Josh. 1:7.) God told them not to turn to the right or the left, so that they might *prosper* wherever they went.

Not Every One Answers the Call

Another fact we can see from Gideon's story is that *everyone who is called will not go.* The first separation that happened in Gideon's army was that those who were afraid were told to go home. (Judges 7:3.) Some Christians today are going to shrink back in fear when the battle is joined. Thirty-five thousand answered the call, but only three hundred made the final count.

This endtime move of God is not for "wimps." The taking of wealth for God's purposes is for those who will rise up and say, "Devil, you've had my stuff long enough. I want you to give it up."

You must get fed up enough to tell the devil, "Enough is enough, and too much is too much."

The Gideon generation will make war in the heavenlies and tear down principalities. They are not asking, but telling, the devil to give up their stuff *now*! When you do that, God will back you up.

God is not going to bring a lot of wealth to an untested and untried person. Proverbs 1:32 says that prosperity in the hand of a fool will destroy him. He wants us to get wisdom about wealth, to learn His purposes, and to be committed to obedience.

He is saying, "Yes, the wealth is there, and it is yours. I have given you the whole earth. But you are not yet ready to take possession."

Why is God still prospering the sinner? As I said before, it is because the Church is not ready to handle the wealth. What would *you* do if God blessed you? Would you remember the first assignment you have from God — to reach the world for Him? Or would you get caught up in buying houses, cars, new clothes, and other "things"?

God is saying to His children on earth, ''I put the wealth in your hands, but you showed Me you did not know how to handle it. So I gave it to the sinner.''

Do not be concerned about how the sinner prospers. Today, you can see evidence on every side that the world system is breaking down. Banks and companies are failing on every hand. The world is becoming frightened of the future. Our nation is in bondage to the banks and money institutions. They are the ones to whom the ''national debt'' is owed — yet they are failing. We are on the verge of bankruptcy as a nation. And, I must say, the Church bears a lot of responsibility for this.

We have not been the ''light of the world'' showing people that God's system works. We have not been the ones doing the most giving to the poor, needy, and homeless. We have not been able, as a majority, to pay our own bills!

Ask the Lord what the Church is doing today that is right, so that He can put the wealth in our hands. God is not going to give things to people who have not proven themselves to be ''good stewards.'' He is not going to give you something that you will misuse.

We think all of the recent scandals have made ''blotches'' on the Church's reputation. We feel so sorrowful because of the way certain leaders have lived that give Christians ''a bad name.'' However, we need to repent for the Church as Daniel did for Israel for something that puts us in a worse light than all of the scandals!

The majority of the Body of Christ is walking in poverty.

That is a terrible reflection on our God. That does not make any sinner out there want to be part of the

Kingdom of God. Why should he change because you say your God is better than the world's — yet he may already be living better than you? However, if you are walking in abundance and debt-free, while he is struggling with bills, you have a talking point about your God.

A "poor" Church presents the idea that the Kingdom is poverty-ridden, and some of the leaders have given the impression that the Church is full of greed. Either way, we have "profaned" God's name before the nations.

> And when they entered unto the heathen, whither they went, they profaned my holy name, when they said to them, These are the people of the Lord, and are gone forth out of his land.
>
> Therefore say unto the house of Israel, Thus saith the Lord God; I do not this for your sakes, O house of Israel, but for mine holy name's sake, which ye have profaned among the heathen, whither ye went.
> **Ezekiel 36:20,22**

God was telling Israel that their sins and idolatry that had brought the curses of the covenant on them causing them to be sent into exile had made His name look bad before the world. They were defeated, poverty-stricken, and captives — yet they called themselves the "people of the one true God." What kind of God was that, the heathen wondered?

He is a God of justice, whose mercy over the people had run out. It was their fault and responsibility that His name was profaned because of their condition. God went on to say that He was going to restore them to Judea *for His name's sake,* not for theirs. He was going to clean them up and take them back in order to "sanctify" His name among the nations. (Ez. 36:23-38.)

Not for your sakes do I do this (v. 32), God said,
be ashamed and confounded for your own ways. He
added:

> Then the heathen that are left round about you
> shall know that I the Lord build the ruined places,
> and plant that that was desolate: I the Lord have
> spoken it, and I will do it.
>
> Ezekiel 36:36

I believe God is going to make this wealth
exchange for *His* name's sake, not because we are so
good and deserving. For hundreds of years now, the
Church has "profaned" His name by teaching that
God wants to keep you poor, that He cannot provide
for you of this world's goods. He only has abundance
in Heaven, we have been taught.

However, in order to restore any truth or anything
of His, God must have a core, a remnant, of people
that will hear and obey what He says to do. He has
ordained that man work in cooperation with Him, so
He gathers a group of His children that can win the
battle — large enough to win but small enough not to
take the credit.

Taking Back Territory

Like me, you probably have heard it preached that
Canaan is a "type of Heaven." But that is not so,
because in Heaven you do not have to "possess"
anything:

*You do not take territory away from the heathen
in Heaven. There are no heathen there. (Rev. 21:27;
22:15.)

*You do not have to fight to get your rightful
"place" or mansion. Jesus has gone to prepare it, and
it will be ready for you. (John 14:2.)

*You do not have to believe or pray for health in Heaven. There is no sickness there — or poverty.

*You do not have to stand on the promises to gain wealth in Heaven. God will provide everything for you in abundance there, because you are His child and a joint-heir with Jesus. (Rom. 8:17.) What is His is yours. It is a gift, not earned.

Canaan is a type of the territory God has allotted you in *this* world. You must fight the "Hittites, Jebusites, Hivites," and so forth to run them out ahead of you. The "ites" are types of demonic strongholds that bind our money, possessions, marriages and families, even our churches.

Jesus won the war, but we have battles still to fight in order to clear the territory allotted to us. God gave Israel the Promised Land, but they still had to "take it back" from the enemy. Of course, if God had not given it, they would not have been able to take it. He fights the battles, but you must make the effort to move out under His direction and follow His commands. (Josh. 5:13-15.)

When Israel first entered the promised land, you will notice that God only let them possess as much as they could handle. The rest He allowed the "ites" to stay on, because the land would have gone to waste if no one was there. Thorns, thistles, and wild animals would have made it necessary for Israel to kill the beasts, reclaim the land, clear it, and restore the soil before they could sow seeds and expect a crop.

Today, that is why God leaves the wealth in the hands of sinners. They are tending certain "patches of ground" and keeping it clean and cultivated for us. That is why I pray for the "Trumps" and "Turners." When it is time for us to possess the wealth of the wicked, all we will have to do is come in and claim it. God will fight the battles.

All you must do is show up for the fight. God told Israel that everything was all ready for them. The cities were built, the vineyards were cultivated, the houses had been erected.

> I will not drive them out from before thee in one year; lest the land become desolate, and the beast of the field multiply against thee.
>
> By little and little I will drive them out from before thee, until thou be increased, and inherit the land.
>
> Exodus 23:29,30

Enlarge your vision to catch hold of this. I am not talking about earth just barely having enough to get by. I am talking about once again the wealth of this earth coming into the hands of the Body of Christ. I am talking about the unsaved world coming to us bringing their wealth.

At this point, the sinner is on the mountaintop where the Church should be. He is calling the shots, telling us what to spend, when to spend it, and where to spend it. We have been forced to be governed by his dictates, but the wealth of the world is *not* for the sinner. It is for us. It is stored up for "the just." That is us.

It is *our* money that they have. God's ultimate plan is to return the wealth to the Church, but if you have a poverty mentality, you will always live below what God has in store for you.

God is wanting to anoint us so that we will have that "touch," so that everything we touch will prosper. Whatever we set our hands to do will be blessed if we keep "covenant" with Him.

Keep therefore the words of this covenant (hear
and obey the word of the Lord), **and do them, that ye
may prosper in all that ye do.**
Deuteronomy 29:9

Perhaps the first place to begin taking back
territory is to get out of debt. When you owe someone,
you are in bondage to that person, bank, or other
institution. God gave His people a promise that they
would lend and not borrow. When you are borrowing,
you do not have dominion. You must have something
in order to rule.

If you owe everyone in town, you cannot rule.
Debt tells you when to work. Creditors rule over you.
They run your life, so to speak. Proverbs 22:7 says that
the borrower is a servant to the lender.

You hear the phrase "we are to be the head and
not the tail" quite often, but there is a *condition* you
do not often hear: to hear God's Word and to do it.

**And the Lord shall open unto thee his good
treasure, the heaven to give the rain unto thy land in
his season, and to bless all the work of thine hand:
and thou shalt lend unto many nations, and thou shalt
not borrow.**

**And *the Lord shall make thee the head, and not
the tail;* and thou shalt be *above only,* and thou shalt
not be beneath;** *if* **that thou hearken unto the
commandments of the Lord thy God, which I
command thee this day, to observe and to do them.**
Deuteronomy 28:12,13

If you want to be "the head" and no longer be
a servant to your creditors, you need to "go by the
manual." The Bible is God's handbook on His
creations. He has set up certain ways for us to go. The
biggest problem with mankind, Christian or not, is that
we have "egos" and think we are smart enough to run
our own lives.

Even educated people are not smart according to God's standards. Education today, at any rate, has become mostly "memorization" and not a real learning process. The "television generation" has to have everything presented in three-minute segments. The average attention span is not long enough in most people to really learn something.

When you begin to study the Word, your mind will begin to be expanded. If you stay in the Bible long enough, you *will* be able to learn, to think and reason, and to operate in the wisdom of God. The Bible is "food" for your soul and spirit. Without food, you become malnourished and eventually starve to death.

Some Christians have little "dwarf" spirits, because they never feed themselves. Meditating on the Word (thinking about it) is the same as digesting food. If you go to service after service and take in all kinds of food, and never digest it, it will not do you any good.

You should immerse yourself in the Word, meditate to digest it, and get to the point that you would be willing to die for it — if you want to be part of "Gideon's army" for this day and time. If you are not willing to die for what you believe, then you really do not believe it yet. I am willing to die for the belief that wealth belongs to God and His people.

The restoration of wealth will be to those who truly believe the whole of the Bible, not just bits and pieces.

14
Wealth Is Not To Keep

Many Christians get caught up in being blessed to the extent that they start to trust in their blessings instead of in God. You can tell this is happening when they begin to "slack off" in church. On Sundays, they are out on the lake in big, new boats, or doing other "fun" things.

God wants you to be cautious about wealth, so that when He begins to bless you, those blessings are not placed ahead of Him. If you do that, you have made an idol out of prosperity. You are living in Babylon rather than in the "Promised Land," as the majority of Jews chose to do at the time of return from exile.

Their eyes had become fixed on prosperity rather than obedience. God had told them through Jeremiah that, if they would accept the exile as from Him, repent, and return to Him, He would prosper them in Babylon. (Jer. 29:4-11.) However, God never meant them to place that prosperity ahead of Him and His plans.

God will not allow anything to be placed ahead of Him in your life.

Trusting in riches is a guaranteed way to fail.

Also, do not promise God things that you do not do. That is called "breaking vows." If God accepts your vow, and provides whatever you have asked for, He expects you to keep your word just as He keeps His.

Sometimes people get so hungry for riches, or so desperate to have a need met, they promise God all sorts of extravagant things. Then, when wealth comes or that need is met, they promptly forget all about those vows. There is a kind of lust that drives some people to do whatever it takes to achieve wealth.

There is a way to get wealth, but God has to call the shots. Jesus said not to even worry about what you would eat, drink, or wear. (Matt. 6:30-32.) That is God's business, not yours. You concentrate on doing the right things, the things God has told you in His Word to do. And all the rest will be given to you.

> **But seek ye first the kingdom of God, and his righteousness; and all these things shall be added unto you.**
>
> **Matthew 6:33**

One man in the Bible was so wrapped up in his riches that he walked away from following Jesus. He made the mistake of thinking that wealth is to keep. He began to trust in the abundance He had. That is a dangerous place to be. This man is called "the rich young ruler" because in one place the Bible calls him "a certain ruler" (Luke 18:18) and in another, a "young man." (Matt. 19:22.)

> **And a certain ruler asked him, saying, Good Master, what shall I do to inherit eternal life?**
>
> **And Jesus said unto him, Why callest thou me good? none is good, save one, that is, God.**
>
> **Thou knowest the commandments, Do not commit adultery, Do not kill, Do not steal, Do not bear false witness, Honour thy father and thy mother.**

**And he said, All these have I kept from my
youth up.**

**Now when Jesus heard these things, he said unto
him, Yet lackest thou one thing: sell all that thou hast,
and distribute unto the poor, and thou shalt have
treasure in heaven: and come, follow me.**

**And when he heard this, he was very sorrowful:
for he was very rich.**

Luke 18:18-23

The last two verses of this story in Matthew are
related this way:

Jesus said unto him, If thou wilt be perfect (the
Greek word means "complete"), **go and sell that thou
hast, and give to the poor, and thou shalt have
treasure in heaven: and come and follow me.**

**But when the young man heard that saying, he
went away sorrowful: for he had great possessions.**
Matthew 19:21,22

Following this incident, Jesus told His disciples it
was easier for a camel to go through the eye of a needle
than for a rich man to enter the kingdom of heaven.
(Matt. 19:23-26; Luke 18:24-27.) Many people
misinterpret Jesus' comments to mean that, if you are
wealthy, you probably cannot go to Heaven.

However, Jesus' real point was that *if you trust in
your riches and are not willing to give them away if He asks,*
then you are making an idol out of your wealth.
Anything you place ahead of God causes you to be into
idolatry and endangers your relationship with God.

He went on to tell His disciples there is no one
who gives up everything for His sake and the Gospel
who will not get back *in this life* a hundred-fold. Also,
He said, that person will have everlasting life. (Matt.
19:29.)

Another rich man who trusted in his wealth would
not even help a beggar who ate the crumbs off his table.

And he took all the credit for making himself wealthy. He was all set to pull down his barns and build larger ones when God required his soul of him. Then he found himself in hell where all of his wealth would not do him any good. (Luke 16:19-31.)

However, all of that does *not* mean wealth is evil. It simply means *trusting in wealth* is evil. The wealth these men had was not the problem. The problem was in their hearts and attitudes: They had made wealth their god. The *love* of money is the root of all evil, the Bible says. (1 Tim. 6:10.) Paul did not write that *money* is the root of evil.

Money must be kept moving, being exchanged for treasures in Heaven — flowing out into the kingdom to accomplish God's purposes and do good — or it is of no value. Once you pile it up into your barns, it ceases to be real wealth, in the terms of the Kingdom of God.

Wealth is not to keep, but to give away, to use for the Kingdom.

One of the saddest things in the world is to see someone work hard all of his life to accumulate wealth and possessions, then die without ever really enjoying it or giving it away for the good of others. The author of Ecclesiastes, called "the preacher," calls that "Vanity, vanity," or "Useless, useless." (Eccl. 1:1-3.)

So when you begin to walk in wealth, make sure you keep your priorities straight. You can become wrapped up in riches and possessions and miss God. You can even miss Heaven.

God Rewards Faithfulness

You also need to understand that no one is going to receive all of the principles in this book, or in the

Word of God, and become a millionaire overnight. Just because you started tithing today does not mean you will have millions tomorrow. God is a God of due process. He rewards faithfulness, continuous service, and a proven heart toward Him.

Look at Abraham, our first example of someone called of God who prospered. Look at how many years it took for the promise of a son to come to pass. The father of the elect — natural and spiritual — did not become a wealthy, prosperous man by the time he got to Haran from Ur of the Chaldees. He prospered over the years gradually, so that when he died, he was extremely wealthy.

Also, Abraham would not receive wealth from anyone who might take the credit for making him rich. He wanted it known that God had prospered him. When he was still Abram, before the fullness of God's promises had come to pass in his life, he won a battle for five kings in the Vale of Siddim but refused all of the spoils they offered him.

> **And Abram said to the king of Sodom, I have lift up mine hand unto the Lord, the most high God, the possessor of heaven and earth,**
>
> **That I will not take from a thread even to a shoelatchet, and that I will not take any thing that is thine, lest thou shouldest say, I have made Abram rich.**
>
> **Save only that which the young men have eaten, and the portion the men which went with me, Aner, Eshcol, and Mamre; let them take their portion.**
> **Genesis 14:22-24**

God releases wealth to come to your house. But you must have a track record. In the world, if you get a raise or if you ask for one, your boss would pull your file, look at your record, and decide whether you deserve one or not. He would look at your production level, your ability to get along with people, and your faithfulness. He would see if you arrived on time, did not leave early, and did not habitually take long lunches.

In spiritual terms, the process is no different. Your track record must be such that God can say, "Yes, he qualifies for this raise. He will handle wealth right. He will remember that it is for giving, and that I provided it."

God needs to see some consistency in the area of giving in your life.

You need to be patient. Do not get anxious simply because you have been "confessing" a few prosperity scriptures for a few months. God is faithful. He will move for you in His time and for His purpose. Some people, eager for money, have wandered from the faith and pierced themselves with many griefs. They did not think God was moving fast enough.

If God blessed you with plenty, would you be like "the rich young ruler"?

If God gave you a Rolls Royce, and at the same time, told you to give it away, could you do it? Could you give it away without even setting foot in it, without driving it one time?

Are you willing to obey God more than having a comparatively short time of luxury? How much do you love the Lord?

John Avanzini, author and teacher on the subject of Biblical finances, has given away many cars. Two of them, he bought new off the showroom floor and never drove. He bought them for missionaries and handed the keys right over to those men. Then he got them back after 90,000 miles had been put on them.

He is a very blessed, well-to-do man, but it all came from God over a period of years of being faithful in obedience and in giving away what God said to give. He has given houses, possessions, and money. His lifestyle is to give.

How attached are you to your possessions? How attached are you to your house or car?

If your heart is all wrapped up in earthly things, that is where your treasure is, and all you will ever have is what you have on earth.

There are few people on earth who do not dream of owning their own homes — their "dream houses." Suppose God suddenly blessed you with the money to build that house. You chose a plan, picked a color scheme, selected the tile, carpet, and draperies, then furnished it with exactly the furniture you always wanted.

Then, before you could live in it, God said, "Give it away. I want you to give it to So-and-so," or perhaps, "Sell it, and give the money to the poor."

Could you do that? That is a major test. Imagine this situation to yourself, and honestly admit whether or not you could do it. If you could not, then you had better deal with some attitudes, for you are not ready for prosperity. This is the situation faced by "the rich young ruler" who went away sorrowful.

Proverbs 11:28 says that the person who trusts in his riches shall fall; and, Proverbs 23:4 warns us not to wear ourselves out to get rich. People who are "workaholics," who work night and day and wear themselves out, usually are those who die building bigger barns and never get to enjoy their wealth.

They wear themselves out and then find health cannot be bought. God initiated "the work ethic" in the Garden of Eden. He assigned Adam not only to have dominion over the earth but to *take care* of everything in the garden — plants, trees, and animals. (Gen. 2:15.) However, when He had to put Adam and Eve out of the garden is when work became hard and tiring, the way we know it today. (Gen. 3:17-19.)

God also instituted a balance from the beginning: One day in seven is supposed to be a rest day. (Gen. 2:2,3)

There is a point my body gets to, then it "shuts down" on me. When I reach that point, I do not push my body any farther. I know it is time to stop and get some rest. After all, my body is the temple of God (1 Cor. 6:19), and I have a responsibility to keep it as healthy as possible.

If you are striving to get rich under your own power, you have a tendency to push your body past the warning signs. Then you become susceptible to all sorts of sicknesses and diseases. There are rich people who die of ill health. If money had been worth their trust, it would have bought them health.

Keep in mind that money is a means to an end, and the *end* is achieving God's results in the earth. Money is a necessary commodity to exchange for things, not to store up where rust and moths corrupt (destroy) and thieves break in to steal. (Matt. 6:19,29.)

God cycles and recycles the wealth of the world to achieve His goals. He simply wants you to be willing to cycle and recycle what you have. He wants you to have your resources ready to give away. You are to be a conduit, not a closed receptacle.

The Process of Exchange

Before God can release wealth into your life, He must know whether you will be faithful and keep Him first in your thoughts. He must know if you can truly follow Jesus, who said, **. . . freely ye have received, freely give** (Matt. 10:8). I understand that, in the context of that verse, Jesus was talking about ministry. However, the principle of giving out what you have received is true in any context.

Look at Psalm 62:10:

> **. . . If riches increase, *set not your heart upon them.***

When you are doing the right thing and being a blessing to people, God will make sure you walk in all kinds of good things. If you give, it *shall* be given to you:

> **Give, and it shall be given unto you; good measure, pressed down, and shaken together, and running over, shall men give into your bosom. For with the same measure that ye mete withal it shall be measured to you again.**
>
> **Luke 6:38**

Proverbs 27:24 says that riches are not forever. That means they could leave at any time. And you could be called to give an account of your soul and leave your riches behind at any time. One thing I have never seen is a U-Haul attached to a hearse!

The Bible says you came into this world naked, and you will go out the same way. (Job 1:21.) Only what you have done for the Lord and, at His instructions, for other people will go with you. In fact, those things precede you. They are the treasures laid up in Heaven. (Matt. 6:19-21.)

God's system is not based on the Dow Jones ratings. Inflation in the world's system does not bother me. If bread costs $90 a loaf, God will see that I have the $90. God is bigger than inflation. Gas prices do not bother me. I have a source that is bigger than the oil cartels.

Jesus said that life is more than food, and the body more than clothes. (Luke 12:22,23.)

> **Therefore I say unto you, Take no thought for your life, what ye shall eat, or what ye shall drink; nor yet for your body, what ye shall put on. Is not the life more than meat, and the body than raiment?**
> **Matthew 6:25**

He was saying in a nice way, "Tend to your own business and leave Mine alone."

He said, "Your Father knows you have need of these things, and He will see that you have them — if doubt and unbelief do not block His provisions from coming to you."

God can take worry out of your life. Also, worry is sin. (Rom. 14:23b — **for whatsoever is not of faith is sin**.) It is better than riches to wake up in the morning and not be worried about anything. That is "riches" for the soul. There are people in the world using drugs and alcohol to take their minds off their problems when all they need to do is come to Jesus, apply the Word, and live the good life.

So you still have bills: Be happy in the middle of them. Things that are seen are subject to change, the Apostle Paul wrote. (2 Cor. 4:18.)

So do not let money of any kind stop with you. Be a channel through which it flows to bless others. *Wealth is not to keep.*

15
Five Obstacles to Blessings

I have touched on some of the hindrances to gaining wealth in earlier chapters, but there are five main obstacles of which you should be aware. They are:

*Laziness.

*Eating up your seed.

*Ignoring sin in your life.

*Giving with the wrong motive or wrong desire.

*Pride.

The first hindrance God showed me to gaining wealth is *laziness.* I cannot find in Scripture one time where God blessed a lazy person. It is one thing to envision things you want to do, but in the meantime, you have to live. Living by faith is fine, but God wants you to put some action with your faith.

Remember that James said, "What does it profit you to say you have faith, if you have no works?" (2:14.)

James also wrote in the last verse of chapter 2: **For as the body without the spirit is dead, so faith without works is dead also.**

The Bible begins with God working, and we are made in His image. He worked six days, then rested "from His labors." (Gen. 2:1-3.)

God gave Adam a job, as I mentioned before.

God said, "I work; you work."

Before the Lord ever gave Adam a wife, He gave him a job — tending the garden.

If a guy wants to marry a girl and tells her he will get a job after the wedding, she had better not fall for that line!

She had better tell him, "No job, no wedding. You are no better than Adam."

During my research on finances, God said to me, "When you get to Revelation, read the future of the Church: it is work."

Revelation 2:26,27 says:

> **And he that overcometh, and keepeth *my works* until the end, to him will I give power over the nations:**
>
> **And he shall rule with a rod of iron; as the vessels of a potter shall they be broken to shivers: even as I received of my Father.**

In 1 Corinthians 6:2,3 Paul asked, "Don't you know the saints will one day judge the world? Don't you know one day you are to judge even angels?"

Making sure the area you are set to govern operates properly is going to be *work*. Kingdom responsibilities on earth already involve hard work. It is work being a pastor, or walking in any of the five-fold offices. However, a pastor's role is probably the hardest, because he deals the most with people.

People are "flaky." Everyone who comes to church is not spiritually mature as yet. Some of them may presume to tell you how to run things. Others may tell you off, and it takes the fruit of the Spirit in abundance to stand there and smile and say, "God bless you, brother," instead of putting your fist in his face.

You think you are going to sit on golden streets, strumming a harp, and talk to Peter and Paul year in and year out through eternity? I have news for you. Revelation says you are to rule and reign on the earth, not sit around Heaven talking with the heroes of faith.

During the Millennium, the earth is going to be a different place. It will be minus Lucifer for a thousand years. (Rev. 20:3.) However, it is going to take a lot of work to straighten things out.

There are many scriptures in the Bible about laziness. Other terms for that condition are *slothful* or "being a sluggard." Proverbs 6:6-8 tells a sluggard to go to the ant for a good example of one who works, does not talk much, and whose fruit speaks for itself.

An ant has no boss always looking over its shoulder to make sure the job is getting done. If someone has to check up on you and push you in order for you to work, you have a serious problem! God said the ant does not need a boss. He is going to do the right thing, the thing he was created to do.

No commander, no overseer, no ruler — yet it stores its provisions in the summer and gathers its food at harvest. If you are always laying around trying not to do anything, the Word says that poverty will come on you like one who travels fast and want will attack you like a bandit. (Prov. 6:11.)

Meantime, the grasshopper in Aesop's little fable based on those verses was having a good time laughing and playing in the summer breezes.

He said, ''Oh, there's lots of time till winter. I'll get around to working next week.'' But ''next week'' never came and winter did.

People who always put things off are not serious about anything.

If you are not working, you should not expect to get anything. But, somehow, lazy people always crave things and resent other people or society if they do not get them. Somehow they never blame themselves because there are things they desire and do not get.

When they avail themselves of what they can do now, then God will give them some of those dreams they have in their hearts.

If God cannot see your faithfulness on an earthly job, how can He trust you with heavenly things? If you are always late, making up excuses to get ''sick leave,'' and taking long lunches, that is not faithfulness. There are many Christians out there, I am sorry to say, who are doing these very things.

Eating up your seed:

Proverbs 23:20 (NASB) says:

> **Do not be with heavy drinkers of wine, or with gluttonous eaters of meat.**

Is that not interesting? The Holy Spirit inspired Solomon to class heavy eaters with heavy drinkers. God put the glutton in the same category as the wino. Both will come to poverty, and drowsiness will clothe that man with rags.

Some people cannot tithe because they eat all of their seed. Some people's grocery bills are as high as their mortgage payments. And you do not have to be fat to be a glutton. I have seen skinny people "wear out a plate or two."

That is literally "eating up your seed." However, if you use your offering money for anything but planting seed, you are "eating up your seed." You might buy anything with it, including paying bills, but that still is using it up and not planting it. You will never get a harvest that way.

Exodus 23:15 says that God's children should not ever come before the Lord empty-handed. Always have something to put in the collection as an offering, a sacrifice of worship, to God.

Ignoring sin in your life:

Proverbs 28:13 says:

He that covereth his sins shall not prosper.

If you are trying to ignore sin in your life and think that because you are giving tithes and offerings, God is going to overlook the sin, you need to read Psalm 66:18:

If I regard iniquity in my heart, the Lord will not hear me.

Perhaps you are thinking, "I have no sin in my heart. I don't smoke, drink, commit adultery, or steal."

However, the Bible's definition of sin does not concern only carnal sins, but also soulish and spiritual. In fact, Paul wrote **for whatsoever is *not of faith* is sin** (Rom. 14:23). *Anything* you do that misses the mark of God's principles, ways, and commandments is sin. That covers a lot of territory!

You could easily get into fear thinking about that, because so very much of what most Christians say, think, and do misses God's standards. However, the

Greek word for *regard* in that verse means "approve of, enjoy, or think about." You might say, then, that *known sin* keeps the Lord from hearing you.

This hindrance to blessing applies in the most part to people who "con" themselves into believing they can continue to do certain things *that they know are wrong* and God will bless them anyway because of their tithes and offerings. This warning applies to those who conceal their sins.

These are the people who come into church, and when the Lord leads the pastor to preach on a certain thing, they think he is preaching *at* them. Then they get mad and leave. If you are trying to cover your sins, prosperity will not find you.

God said that, if you would confess your sins, He would forgive you. (1 John 1:9.) However, some people try to manipulate God like a puppet on a string. You cannot use 1 John 1:9 to justify *premeditated* sin. When you confess your sins, do not go back and do them again.

Some Christians think they can keep on doing wrong things, thinking wrong thoughts, and saying wrong things, and yet, God will forgive them over and over. That will not happen, if you are deliberately continuing to do those things. God's grace covers you if you are making genuine efforts to change.

The one who confesses *and forsakes* his sin finds mercy, according to Proverbs 28:13. If all you are doing is playing games with God's grace, you will have serious problems.

Corporate Sin Can Affect You

Also, "corporate sins" can affect you, as we saw earlier in the story of Achan, who kept forbidden things out of greed. God spoke to Joshua as if the entire nation had sinned. (Josh. 7.) They lost a battle, and when Joshua and the elders sought the Lord, He said:

Israel hath sinned, and they have also transgressed my covenant which I commanded them.
Joshua 7:11

And, as I also wrote in an earlier chapter, I believe the Church's shortcomings and failures have affected not only members of the Body but this entire nation.

What you do even affects the rest of the people in your local church. We are all part of one body. Only when Achan's sin was addressed and judgment fell on him and his household were the Israelites able to continue on to victory. That is why God has been "cleaning house" for the past few years. He cannot take even "Gideon's army" on to victory as long as rampant sin runs in the leaders. Next, I believe He will bring sanctification throughout the Body.

The old saying, "No man is an island," is very, very true. You affect the brothers and sisters around you. That is the corporate anointing. That is why God has begun to set order once again in the Church. There must be restoration of order, obedience, and respect for Him, before He can restore blessings.

When God judges a nation, He judges everyone in it. One of the saddest stories in the Bible is when Abraham interceded for Sodom and Gomorrah, but God could not find even ten righteous people in it. However, it is comforting to know that God is willing to withhold judgment for the sake of the righteous.

We live in a nation today that has shook its fist in God's face and said, "We do not need God. *We* are gods. We are superior in ourselves."

Society today makes decisions that rightfully are only God's to make. Americans as a society are usurping divine authority when abortion is legal and euthanasia (killing the terminally ill and permitting suicide) is condoned.

If it were not for the righteous in our country, this nation already would be just part of history — another fallen "empire." American society today is *worse* than Sodom and Gomorrah.

Just because you and I, and many other Christians, are living right does not mean this nation can escape some judgment. Even if enough righteous can be found to spare it from utter destruction, we already are coming under the "curses," the consequences of breaking God's covenant.

America was started as a "covenant nation." Even before the Revolutionary War, the pilgrims on the Mayflower made a covenant with God for this new continent and nation. As long as the majority of Americans honored that, we escaped most of the curses.

In this century, however, America has more and more turned away from God and toward the idea that "man is god" (secular humanism). Even two world wars and a great depression did not cause the nation to return to God. Today, we are having crop failures, animals not bearing as they should, increasing natural disasters, an epidemic of fear, and plagues (AIDS). All of those you will find in Leviticus 26 and Deuteronomy 28.

America has become a covenant-breaking nation. The only hope we have is to repent for the nation as Daniel did for Judah and for God to raise up "Gideon's army" for our time.

Wrong Motives, Wrong Desires:

The next category of major hindrances to blessings is a mindset that almost all Americans have, even Christians It is the "me syndrome," the focusing on self that has become increasingly a part of our society and our thinking since the Sixties.

We focus on what we want, on "our" rights regardless of others' rights, and on what will entertain us, pleasure us, and make us feel that we are okay.

James 4:3 says that you ask but do not receive because you want things from God for your own "lusts." If you have asked God for something but not received, better examine your motives and your desires. Is your motive for asking selfish, self-centered, and self-seeking?

Do you want whatever it is to make you "feel good" in some way? Or do you want it for God's purposes? Do you want it to be able to serve Him better? Are you seeking for something to bring more luxury, more pleasure, or for vanity's sake?

If your motives and desires are wrong, God will not let wealth come into your hands — or, if it does, you will not keep it long.

Ephesians 4:22-24 tells us the proper occupation of a Christian: to put off "the old man" (the old nature which is like the world) and to put on "the new man" (which is conforming to the image of Jesus). You cannot put on the new man — which means bringing the soul and body into line with the new spirit man God has given you at conversion — if you still think, talk, and act like the world.

Studying the Word, developing a fellowship with the Holy Spirit, and hearing the Word preached and taught as part of a local body are the only ways in which you can "put on the new man." And, I must tell you, the new man is the one who receives the blessings.

Ephesians 5:1 says for us, His dearly loved children, to imitate God.

Why do you want wealth? Do you just want to have bigger cars and houses, better clothes and food? I am not against nice cars, houses, and possessions. But, remember, to enjoy wealth for yourself is the *last* part of the three-fold purpose of wealth. The other two parts must come first.

To accomplish God's purposes in the world and in your life and to help others must be your first desire and your main motive for desiring wealth. You come last, and actually, that part is not even your business. (Matt. 6:25-34.) You should not be desiring wealth for that last part. Set your desires on wealth for the first two reasons, and God will see that your needs, personal desires, and enjoyment are fulfilled.

The purpose of wealth is not *you*. Many Christians stand on the brink of receiving today, but they will not receive unless they change their priorities for receiving. God is responsible for you, and He does not mind you having fine things. But He looks at your faith and obedience. He looks at how many works go with your faith. He looks at your *faithfulness*.

"Works" cannot earn you salvation or eternal life. However, they do determine your blessings and rewards *if* they are done with the right attitude (willing) and the right motive (to be obedient and please the God whom you love better than anything else in the world).

John Avanzini, teacher and writer on God's financial principles, says that Jesus is Lord only to those who do His will and not their own wills. Jesus is our perfect pattern to follow. Remember that we are to be channels through which wealth can flow, not closed vaults where it stays.

God will give wealth to those who understand that it is His and not theirs.

The last big obstacle to wealth that I want to discuss is:

Pride:

Be very, very careful of pride. Evidence speaks for itself. You do not have to go around bragging about what you have. Be sure your "testimonies" are to God and not to *your* faith or your good reputation. Boasting can be a dangerous trap. You can begin to have "faith in your faith" instead of faith in God.

Pride, self-will, and rebellion are the three basic characteristics of Lucifer, and they carry over into the old nature, the Adamic nature of fallen man. Solomon wrote that when pride comes, then cometh shame. (Prov. 11:2.) So, if you get into pride over the things God has done for you, before too long, you probably will experience shame.

In the list of seven things that God hates and that are an abomination to him, *a proud look* is the first one listed. (Prov. 6:16.)

In Proverbs 22:4, Solomon wrote that *humility and reverence* (for God) are what brings wealth. A humble person will not elevate himself because of what God does, nor will he begin to worship creation (things) instead of the Creator, as Paul wrote that mankind in general had done. (Rom. 1:25.)

Many Christians still have a lot of pride in them. They will not work at just any job, for example. Many of them have to hunt prestigious jobs. Also, many who are called into the ministry cannot be themselves. Pride keeps them from thinking they are good enough. So they "prostitute" someone else's anointing.

You quite often see "little Copelands or Hagins or Benny Hinns" out there in the ministry, trying to wear someone else's identity because that person is very successful. Be yourself. God has no one else like you, and He wants you to be what He has designed for you to be. What is wrong with being a pioneer?

You need to remember one thing about wealth: It is useless in the day of wrath. Seek it for what you can do with it for God, because on judgment day, it will do you no good. All you can take with you is what you did for God and other people.

Ecclesiastes 5:10 says that the person who loves money never has enough of it. Solomon said it was "vanity" to seek after the world's goods for their own sake.

Seek wealth for God's sake.

16

The Restoration of Wealth

God is speaking a "word in due season" (Prov. 15:23) to those who will listen, whose ears are open to hear the Word of the Lord. The Bible says that God does not come in "wind, earthquake, or fire." (1 Kings 19:11,12.) He comes as "a still small voice."

I have learned to move when I hear that voice. When you know the voice of the Lord, you move on it, and to learn His voice, you must spend some time with Him.

God said to us in a word of prophecy, "I am going to restore wealth to My people. I am going to manifest My glory through them. There is coming a separation between My people and the world. And it will be a distinct separation. Many shall come to My people to observe and ask them how it is done."

You need to be ready to give the world an answer in due season. You need to know what God is doing and why. In these days, God wants us to get past the excitement of the anointing and begin to ask Him what we should do with it. The anointing is not there to make your flesh feel good, but to do ministry.

You should not be satisfied with "experience." You need to know why the experience comes and what you should do with it.

One of the things the Church is going to be known for in the last days is the glory of God. The Bible says that we are "the light of the world." (Matt. 5:14.) That means we are supposed to be shining outside the walls of our churches.

You should "shine" the brightest away from church. It is easy to get in agreement with God and His people during the service. What counts is what you do outside the Christian community. Is your light shining bright? Can the world see God in you?

Every Christian has a "church light" of some kind, but what about a "world light"? The glory is to be on His people in days to come. I am seeing already that God is making a distinction between the Church and the world. He is beginning to bring His people to a different plateau of existence.

Most of us need to realize that we are born eagles but are living like chickens. We need to be looking down on circumstances, not up at them. When the storms come, the eagle flies above them. He lets his wings carry him above the situation. I am talking about living on the mountaintop where the high call is — because *that is where the restoration is.*

I have been to the mountaintop, and I am pregnant with vision. I go into my times of prayer and see these things, but when I come out and try to explain them, sometimes people look at me funny. Not everyone can see the vision from the mountain. But there is a place you can walk in Jesus, where no one will have to ask if you are saved. They will see the glory on you.

Have you had people knocking on your door asking how you are doing it? I doubt it. However, when God begins to restore the wealth to His people, sinners are going to marvel at the blessings and come from near and far to find out how this is happening.

If you are looking at jobs and economic conditions as your source of income and your assurance that you are safe, I guarantee you are coming to a time when you will be depressed and "shook up." If your trust is not in the Lord, you are going to have serious problems. There is *no* answer but God. The world has no answers, otherwise it would not be in the condition it is now.

I issue altar calls for non-tithers to give people attending my church the opportunity to get right with God so when the blessings begin to flow, they will not be on the outside looking in.

There is no lack in God. He is our "Daddy." Most of the time, before your children come and tell you about needs they have, you already see them, do you not? You may have already made plans to meet those needs. Do you think God is not as good a parent as you are?

He sees your needs and already was making some moves before you knew it. However, remember that He is moved by faith and not needs. Just let Him be God, believe His Word, and He will come up with the resources. Why should I worry about how my needs are to be met, when that is His job? (Matt. 6:25-34.) Simply seek Him and what He wants you to do first, then your needs will be met.

The purpose of a job is not to put food on your table or clothes on your back. The purpose of a job is to have something to give. James wrote that if all you ever do is talk without meeting the needs of people, your talking is all in vain.

> **What doth it profit, my brethren, though a man say he hath faith, and have not works? can faith save him?**
>
> **If a brother or sister be naked, and destitute of daily food,**
>
> **And one of you say unto them, Depart in peace, be ye warmed and filled; notwithstanding ye give them not those things which are needful to the body; what doth it profit?**
>
> **James 2:14-16**

If you use your income for the right purpose, God will make sure you never lack anything. Basically, God made life to be simple. He carries the burden. All we are to do is hear and obey. Once you understand that life is not complicated, you will go through the church doors praising God.

When I learned that life is simply *choices you make*, it "blessed my socks off." You choose to obey, or not to obey. You choose to do what is right in the sight of God, or you choose to "do your own thing." The results depend on your choices.

Most of the time, we make wrong choices — then blame God for our choices not being right. God will not violate your right to choose. He gives you an alternative, and you have to weigh the evidence to see which way you are going to go. Finally, you make a decision. Based on that decision, the consequences are good or bad for you.

People Will Give To You Willingly

Look at what Isaiah wrote about restoration in chapter 61. These are the verses that Jesus quoted in his hometown of Nazareth when He stood up to teach in the synagogue. (Luke 4:16-21.) The first two verses He read really were a proclamation that He was

Messiah, and He stopped at the first phrase of Isaiah 61:2, which says: **To proclaim the acceptable year of the Lord.** (Luke 4:19.)

We are still living in that ''acceptable year.'' We are still living in restoration, and the restoration of wealth has been waiting for its due time. The rest of that second verse speaks of the ''day of vengeance of our God.'' Praise the Lord that we are not yet to that day. But let's see what restoration Jesus came to do in this ''acceptable year.''

> **And they shall build the old wastes, they shall raise up the former desolations, and they shall repair the waste cities, the desolations of many generations.**
>
> **And strangers shall stand and feed your flocks, and the sons of the alien shall be your plowmen and your vinedressers.**
>
> **But ye shall be named the Priests of the Lord: men shall call you the Ministers of our God: ye shall eat the riches of the Gentiles** (nations who are not of God), **and in their glory shall ye boast yourselves.**
>
> **For your shame** (because of the shame you have suffered) **ye shall have double; and for confusion they shall rejoice in their portion: therefore in their land they shall possess the double: everlasting joy shall be unto them.**
>
> **For as the earth bringeth forth her bud, and as the garden causeth the things that are sown in it to spring forth; so the Lord God will cause righteousness and praise to spring forth before all the nations.**
>
> **Isaiah 61:4-7,11**

Verse 6 says that God's people will feed on the wealth of nations and boast in their riches. We are not going to have to take it from them. They are going to willingly give it to us. Just rest in the Lord, do the right thing, and people will give into your bosom. (Luke 6:38.) People's hearts will be turned toward blessing you.

God was saying, ''There is coming a time when My people will receive a double portion instead of shame, and instead of disgrace, they will rejoice in their inheritance. All who see them will acknowledge this is a people whom God has blessed.''

Ecclesiastes says a poor man's wisdom is soon forgotten (Eccl. 9:15,16), but the world will acknowledge that *the* God is your God by the abundance of things that you have.

The book of Joel also talks about the process of restoration.

> Be glad then, ye children of Zion, and rejoice in the Lord your God: for he hath given you the former rain moderately, and he will cause to come down for you the rain, the former rain, and the latter rain in the first month.
>
> And the floors shall be full of wheat, and the vats shall overflow with wine and oil.
>
> And I will restore to you the years that the locust hath eaten, the cankerworm, and the caterpillar, and the palmerworm, my great army which I sent among you.
>
> And ye shall eat in plenty, and be satisfied, and praise the name of the Lord your God, that hath dealt wondrously with you: and my people shall never be ashamed.
>
> Joel 2:23-27

Many people think those verses are for natural Israel, but the Apostle Peter on the Day of Pentecost said those words were beginning to be fulfilled that day. In Acts 2:16-21, Peter quoted the next two verses as proof the days of restoration were beginning:

> And it shall come to pass afterward (after Jesus came to destroy the works of Satan and restore all things), that I will pour out my spirit upon all flesh;

and your sons and your daughters shall prophesy, your old men shall dream dreams, your young men shall see visions:

And also upon the servants and upon the handmaids in those days will I pour out my spirit.

Zion was a term used for Jerusalem, and in Galatians, Paul wrote that the born-again descendants of Abraham were the children of Jerusalem. (Gal. 4:22-31.) Those promises of restoration in Isaiah 61 are to the children of Zion.

Already we have seen how God's principle of restoration relates to individuals. When Job got his thinking straightened out and repented, God restored twice what had been taken from him. The Lord also will "turn your captivity," when you do what Job did.

Restoration is coming for those whose hearts are right. I am not talking only about wealth. I believe restoration is coming in many marriages and families. The moment you take your hands off and turn things over to God, He can begin to work. If you let Him do it, it will all work out.

Look at what Amos wrote about restoration:

Behold, the days are coming, saith the Lord, that the plowman shall overtake the reaper, and the treader of grapes him that soweth seed; and the mountains shall drop sweet wine, and all the hills shall melt.

Amos 9:13

That verse says that, before you get the seed in the ground, harvest will be staring you in the face. I wrote earlier about the time between planting and harvest. However, God said there is coming a day when almost as soon as you plant, the harvest will be ready.

Those of you who have been sowing seeds for a while may suddenly find yourself harvesting almost before you can plant more.

About the Author

Wilson D. Douglas III is the founder and pastor of Agape Christian Center in League City, Texas.

He and his wife, Elizabeth Ann, have one daughter, Ashley Nicole. God called him into the ministry in 1982 after two years of building a solid foundation in his life.

The thrust of Douglas' present ministry, which began in 1986, is to teach "victorious living" to the Body of Christ. *Victorious Living* also is the name of the ministry's television program. Because of the musical ability God has given Douglas, he writes, plays, and sings praise and worship songs that deal with victorious, successful living and with the Person of the Holy Spirit.

One of the unique things about this ministry is that all of the ministry tools are given away (books, tapes, Bibles, and so forth). And, in return, God has supplied all of their needs. The ministry is known as "a place of hope and victory in a difficult world for all types, kinds, and classes of people."

To contact the author,
write:

Wilson D. Douglas III
Agape Christian Center
P. O. Box 1315
League City, TX 77574

For additional copies
of *Wealth God's Way,*
contact:

VINCOM Inc.
P. O. Box 702400
Tulsa, OK 74170

918-254-1276

Notes

Notes

Notes

Notes

Notes

Notes

Notes

Notes

Notes